Praise for *Rainmaking Conversations*

"*Rainmaking Conversations* is the ultimate strategic guide to creating dialogs so valuable that they rise above the noise, create engagement, and make you the anchor others must unseat in order to compete."

—Ardath Albee, Author of *eMarketing Strategies for the Complex Sale*

"*Rainmaking Conversations* is the one sales book you should absolutely read if you want to become a top sales performer while also maintaining the highest integrity."

—Paige Arnof-Fenn, Founder and CEO, Mavens & Moguls LLC

"*Rainmaking Conversations* hits upon an eternal truth: that despite the technology, the complexity, and the noise that surrounds us today, sales arise from a dialog between two people. But it doesn't just theorize and observe, it presents a practical, step-by-step guide to developing the psychology, skills, knowledge, and processes necessary to excel at winning new business. If you put into practice just half of the ideas in this book, you'll never struggle with sales again."

—Ian Brodie, Managing Director, Rainmaker Academy

"Those who can't make rain think it's about luck and personality. Real rainmakers know that it's about hard work, preparation, and proven methods. Except for the hard work, everything you need is in this book."

—Thomas H. Davenport, Author of *Competing on Analytics*

"In [a] commoditized world, value is the key differentiator. And the brain trust at the RAIN Group has done it again. This isn't a book—it's a symphony.

They provide daily practices that anyone who sells can implement into their efforts immediately. Read this book and you won't just make it rain, you'll make it POUR!"

—Scott "The Nametag Guy" Ginsberg, Professional Speaker, and Author of *How to Be That Guy*

"Trust drives sales, and conversations drive trust. Really great salespeople have conversations that create trust, with sales as the natural outcome. *Rainmaking Conversations* is a how-to book that goes way beyond tactics; it's about integrating trust, relationship, and sales."

—Charles Green, Founder and CEO, Trusted Advisor Associates, and Author of *Trust-Based Selling*

"Today's crazy-busy prospects won't waste their time with you unless they get value from every interaction. In *Rainmaking Conversations*, you'll learn how to make that a reality."

—Jill Konrath, Author of *SNAP Selling and Selling to Big Companies*

"There are too many books on selling but once in a while one comes along with a fresh approach. This one is worth reading even by the seasoned professional."

—Philip Kotler, S.C. Johnson & Son Distinguished Professor of International Marketing, Kellogg School of Management, Northwestern University

"While many books exist on related subjects, *Rainmaking Conversations* provides a fresh and well thought out strategic sales path from "hello" to "let's get started" for all of us who are committed to growing our organizations. Kudos to Schultz and Doerr on this compelling read. Let it RAIN!"

—David Lissy, CEO, Bright Horizons Family Solutions

"Schultz and Doerr have given us a perfect prescription for profitable selling. They've zeroed in on exactly what it takes to be a rainmaker—the sales conversation. The chapter on value propositions alone is worth more than the price of the book. Don't think twice. Buy this book. Read it, apply it, and watch your sales success soar."

—Michael W. McLaughlin, Author of *Winning*
the Professional Services Sale

"In the hypercompetitive world of selling and all the expert opinions floating around it, Schultz and Doerr present an eloquent 'thinking person's guide' to long-term success in building and maintaining successful customer relationships. If you believe that excellence in sales and service are not mutually exclusive, that buying trumps selling and listening outweighs talking, your world view will be highly receptive to the lessons they teach regarding the required competence, preparation, and skills for professional selling success. If not, find a new career."

—Peter Ostrow, Research Director, Sales Effectiveness,
Aberdeen Group

"There are lots of books on selling but few as free of fluff as *Rainmaking Conversations*. Read it and you'll see a clear, convincing, and compelling case for how to sell in virtually any situation. Kudos to Schultz and Doerr for writing such a valuable book. Highly recommended."

—Michael Port, *New York Times* **Best-Selling Author of** *Book*
Yourself Solid

"Buyers choose to do business with people they like. True rainmaking, the kind that makes you 5 or even 10 times more successful than the plodding average, comes from mastering conversations with buyers. In this book—chock-full of compelling stories and winning techniques—Mike Schultz and John Doerr show you how to master the art of rainmaking."

—David Meerman Scott,
Best-Selling Author of *The New Rules of Marketing & PR*

"Nothing happens without sales . . . and Mike Schultz and John Doerr have effectively provided us all with the book on sales that will make things happen! *Rainmaking Conversations* is a must read!"

—Leonard A. Schlesinger, President, Babson College

"I love this book. Why? Because *Rainmaking Conversations* isn't yet another collection of empty tips-and-tricks calories that provides no real nourishment to your career. It is, on the other hand, a compelling, interesting, far-reaching, and highly relevant guide to being who you need to be, and precisely how you need to do what you need to do, to be among the elite, that top 10 percent of sales professionals who are 'The Rainmakers.' Folks, take it from me. This is the real thing."

—Dave Stein, CEO and Founder, ES Research Group, Inc.

"In *Rainmaking Conversations*, Mike Schultz and John Doerr give a practical and inspiring set of action steps to preparing ourselves for sales success. What a thorough and accessible program they have laid out here! No fluff, no abstractions, plenty of meaty anecdotes. This book provides a solid to-do list for professionals who want to get more business without flailing around."

—Ruth P. Stevens, President, eMarketing Strategy, and Adjunct Professor of Marketing, Columbia Business School

RAINMAKING
CONVERSATIONS

RAINMAKING
CONVERSATIONS

INFLUENCE, PERSUADE,
AND SELL IN ANY SITUATION

MIKE SCHULTZ
JOHN E. DOERR

WILEY

John Wiley & Sons, Inc.

Published by John Wiley & Sons, Inc., Hoboken, New Jersey.

Published simultaneously in Canada.

For general information on our other products and services or for technical support, please contact our Customer Care Department within the United States at (800) 762-2974, outside the United States at (317) 572-3993 or fax (317) 572-4002.

Wiley also publishes its books in a variety of electronic formats. Some content that appears in print may not be available in electronic books. For more information about Wiley products, visit our web site at www.wiley.com.

Library of Congress Cataloging-in-Publication Data:

Schultz, Mike, 1974–

    Rainmaking conversations : influence, persuade, and sell in any situation / Mike Schultz, John E. Doerr.

        p. cm.

    ISBN 978-0-470-92223-1 (cloth)

    ISBN 978-1-118-02575-8 (ebk)

    ISBN 978-1-118-02576-5 (ebk)

    ISBN 978-1-118-02577-2 (ebk)

        1. Selling—Psychological aspects. 2. Persuasion (Psychology) 3. Influence (Psychology) I. Doerr, John E. II. Title.

    HF5438.8.P75S36 2011

    658.85—dc22

                                                              2010045649

Printed in the United States of America

10 9 8 7 6 5 4 3 2 1

To Erica.

—MES

To Chris, John Michael, and Andrew.

—JED

Contents

Acknowledgments

In order for this book and any of our books to come to fruition, a number of people have to continue to do the real work so we can take the time to write. For that, we'd like to acknowledge our colleagues at RAIN Group and RainToday.com: Bob Croston, Erica Stritch, Mark Fortune, Mary Flaherty, Michelle Davidson, Adam Tokarz, Kelly Kerr, Zach Rachins, John Michael Doerr, Terese Riordan, Jae-ann Rock, Jim Miller, Sandy O'Dell, and Sue Brisson for keeping everything moving forward. Thanks especially to our internal editors John Michael Doerr and Erica Stritch who were not afraid to tell us when we needed to go back to the drawing board and rewrite until it was just right. This book is infinitely better due to their willingness to push, prod, and cajole. Thanks to Scott Whipple for his fine work in preparing the graphics for the book.

We'd also like to thank Mike Treske (John Hancock Annuities Distribution, John Hancock Wood Logan), Nicole Giantonio (Buck Consultants, a Xerox Company), John Calucci (McLane, Graf, Raulerson & Middleton, PA), John Flavin (Edgewater Technology), Dan Cohen (Linkage), Lilian Eilers (The Blue Ocean Company), Marcus de Layen Vian (IRIS Software and Services), Marisa Edmund (Edmund Optics), Mike Sheehan (Hill Holliday), Jim Keenan (Pace), Mark Gowrie (AchieveGlobal), David Carrithers (Centennial Contractors), Richard Wetenhall (formerly Mercer and McKinsey), Kevin Davis (Topline Leadership), Jere Doyle (Prospectiv) and Deborah Dumaine (Better Communications) who generously gave their time to lend their thoughts and experiences to the content of the book.

To Dave Kurlan and Rocky LaGrone (Objective Management Group) thanks for your thoughtful insight into what it take to be a true rainmaker.

To our valued clients, we repeatedly thank you for the privilege of working with you and accepting us as members of your teams. To the authors, contributors, members, and readers of RainToday.com, we appreciate your continued support, content, questions, and interactions with us through the years.

We are also grateful to our editor at John Wiley & Sons, Inc., Daniel Ambrosio, along with Ashley Allison and Lauren Freestone, who once again helped us keep on target through the editing process, and to everyone else at John Wiley & Sons, Inc., who helped see this book to its final form.

—Mike Schultz and John Doerr

I can never thank my mom, Gloria Doerr, enough. She continues to inspire me and everyone else in our ever-expanding extended family with her ability to stay young and work hard even at 84 years. (Sorry, Mom, everyone knows your age by now.) I also want to thank my in-laws Jeff, Al, Rob, Jessica, and Randy, who were not mentioned by name in our first book but should have been. Of course, I continue to draw strength from the warmth and caring of my sisters Jean, Judi, Jen, and Jodi, and my brother Jim and all their children, in-laws, and grandchildren. And to my friends who have become a part of that family. I am what I am because of all of you.

A special thanks to Over the Hill Basketball and my friends on the court. As we have heard repeatedly, it is this twice-a-week activity that keeps us off the streets and more fun to be around. It certainly does that and so much more for me.

Finally, to my wife, Chris, and to my sons, John Michael and Andrew, who continue to provide love and support—and that's all that matters.

—John Doerr

To my wife and best friend, Erica Schultz, each day we spend together is a joy and a privilege. And to my family, Stan, Nancy, Marvin, Linda, Allyson, Mike, Mikey, Mikayla, Dave, Alena, Shirley, and everyone else. For your continued love and support, I can't thank you enough.

—Mike Schultz

PART ONE

GETTING READY TO MAKE RAIN

1 | Introduction

Ideal conversation must be an exchange of thought, and not, as many of those who worry most about their shortcomings believe, an eloquent exhibition of wit or oratory.

—Emily Post

It's 4 PM on a Thursday and you're about to meet the CEO of a major company you'd like to win as a client. The conversation starts as you walk into the office, approach the CEO, stretch out your hand, and say, "Nice to meet you, Jill. I'm Steve Webb."

Fast forward to a meeting about four months later—3 PM on a Wednesday this time. You head into the office. Jill gets out from behind her desk and says, "Good to see you again, Steve. Here's the check for $1.2 million that you need to get the process underway. Let's schedule the kickoff for next Friday."

Suffice it to say, a lot has to happen between "nice to meet you" and "here's a check for $1.2 million." Yet two things are true:

1. This *is* how it happens.
2. Conversations form the bridge between "hello" and "let's go."

As sales trainers, sales managers, and sellers ourselves, we've had the privilege of observing and analyzing thousands of telephone and face-to-face sales conversations. All too often we see salespeople say "hello," but never get to "let's go," because of mistakes they make in

3

their conversations. We also regularly see salespeople unable to generate the conversations they need. Limited sales conversations = limited sales opportunities.

We wrote *Rainmaking Conversations: Influence, Persuade, and Sell in Any Situation* for salespeople, business leaders, professionals, and anyone who wants to create and lead masterful sales conversations—conversations that fill the pipeline, win new deals, and create the greatest opportunities for the largest, most secure, and most profitable accounts.

If this is what you want to do, *Rainmaking Conversations* is for you.

RAIN, RASP, and 10 Rainmaker Principles

RAIN, RASP, and the 10 Rainmaker Principles form the core of the RAIN Selling method—the training and development program we at RAIN Group employ to help companies create dramatic improvements in sales performance and to help individuals become top-performing rain-makers. We cover a number of topics throughout the book, all to help you have the most and best sales conversations, and all connected to RAIN, RASP, and the 10 Rainmaker Principles.

RAIN—Your Guide to Rainmaking Conversations

RAIN is an acronym for Rapport, Aspirations and Afflictions, Impact, and New Reality. These concepts are the core concepts you need to remember to lead a rainmaking conversation. In addition, the "A" and the "I" perform double duty, standing for *Advocacy* and *Inquiry*, and the "IN" will help you to remember to maximize your *Influence*. The RAIN acronym is also a nod to the fact that this process is focused on *rainmakers*—a common name for people who bring the most new clients and revenue into an organization. RAIN is the central theme of the book and is your guide to leading successful sales conversations.

Graphically, RAIN looks like Figure 1.1.

R is Rapport—Chapter 5: The ability to build rapport in sales conversations is an old concept that is more relevant and more important than ever. At the same time, rapport is talked about less and less in the sales training

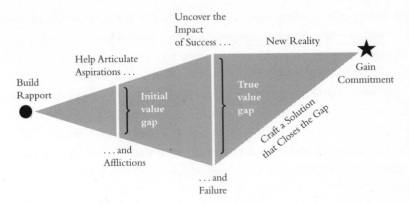

Figure 1.1   RAIN Selling

community, often dismissed as a ploy to make a superficial connection with a potential customer. We agree—you shouldn't make superficial connections, you should make *genuine* connections. Genuine rapport sets the foundation for the rest of the conversation, and creates the opportunity for trust and a strong relationship.

A genuine connection with a potential client is so important in selling because, all things being equal, buyers tend to buy from—and allow themselves to be influenced by—people they like. Rapport is an often-overlooked factor that can tip the scales in favor of one seller over another throughout the buying process: from who gets in the game at the beginning, to who is allowed to move along in the process, and even to who eventually wins.

> I have always really liked this adage: "Nobody really cares how much you know until they know how much you care." We try to drill people as much as possible to the idea of listening, absorbing, and really understanding so you, as a salesperson, can make the deepest connection and learn how you can help them the most.
>
> —Mike Treske, President, John Hancock Annuities Distribution, John Hancock Wood Logan

A is Aspirations and Afflictions—Chapter 6: The "A" in RAIN Selling stands for Aspirations and Afflictions. Many sales methodologies suggest that to sell products and services as solutions to needs, you must first uncover the problems or pain of the potential client. Focusing only on problems and pain (afflictions) can do sellers a disservice because problems and pain are only half of the story.

When customers buy, they are typically thinking as much about Aspirations (the future they are seeking) as they are about Afflictions (problems they'd like to fix). If you think about asking questions only in the negative, you will tend to probe for needs that way. You'll tend to ask questions such as, "Where are you unhappy with performance?," "What keeps you up at night?,"[1] and "What are your problems?" Think of Aspirations as much as Afflictions, and you will remember to ask future-seeking as well as problem-solving questions—questions with themes like "Where do you want to go?" and "What are the possibilities?" If you ask questions that look to the future, you will find that—instead of just bringing some Advil for the pain—you will be able to paint the most compelling, impactful, and comprehensive vision of a new and better reality for your clients.

Free RAIN Selling Resources Online

There's only so much space in any book, but there's so much to share with you to help you master the art of rainmaking conversations.

Thus, we've made numerous tools, resources, and additional learning content available to you on www.rainsalestraining.com/booktools.

Also, on the book-tools page, we've made lessons of our popular RAIN Selling training online free to you as a buyer of this book. We hope you find these additional resources helpful to your quest to succeed with your sales conversations and overall.

Free RAIN Selling resources: www.rainsalestraining.com/booktools

---

[1] You'll find advice to ask the question "What keeps you up at night?" here and there scattered about sales books and sales advice materials. The concept is good to keep in mind, but don't ask the question verbatim like this. It's a cliché, and it usually comes across as contrived.

I is Impact—Chapter 7: After you uncover a prospect's aspirations and afflictions, the question then becomes, "So what?" If your afflictions don't get solved, then so what? What won't happen? Will they get worse? How will they affect the bottom line of your company, division, or department? How will they affect your life?

If your aspirations don't become reality, so what? In a business-to-business scenario, the questions that follow might sound like, "Will your competition get ahead of you if you don't innovate?," "Will you lose market share if you aren't aggressive in your strategy?," "Will you never be able to grow your business to a point where you can sell it and reach your personal financial goals?," and "Will the promotion you so desire continue to elude you?"

The exact "so what" questions will vary depending on the situation, but your ability to quantify and paint the "so what" picture is the foundation for how important it is for the decision maker to buy from you. This is of paramount importance to you, because although your competition is often another provider, about 23.6 percent of sales that are forecasted by companies to close end in no decision at all.[2] Lack of impact leads to lack of urgency to make a decision. This leads to delays. Time kills sales.[3]

Creating urgency for buying hinges on how well you help your client answer the "so what" questions, and how well you demonstrate the impact of buying from you.

N is New Reality—Chapter 8: One of the greatest difficulties in sales is helping prospects to understand exactly what they get when they work with you. Clients need an argument to justify the benefit to themselves and to other people involved in the buying decision. At the end of a well-managed sales process, your job is to create a vision of a New Reality that will be the best for your client, given their specific Aspirations and Afflictions and the Impact of doing (or not doing) something about them.

---

[2] J. Dickie and B. Trailer, "2010 Sales Performance Optimization: Sell Cycle Review Analysis," p. 28.

[3] Time kills sales because of the Law of Diminishing Intent. This states that the longer a person waits to make a decision, the less enthusiasm they will have for the idea, and the less likely the decision will be a yes.

> It's not selling someone something they don't want. It's about talking about their needs and positioning what you have to fulfill their needs.
>
> —Nicole Giantonio, Vice President, Sales, Buck Consultants, a Xerox Company

A and I is Advocacy and Inquiry—Chapter 9: In RAIN, the "A" stands for Aspirations and Afflictions, and the "I" stands for Impact. The "A" and the "I" also help us to remember to balance Advocacy and Inquiry.

Many inexperienced salespeople believe their job is show and tell. And tell. And tell. Incessant pitching and presenting feels to buyers like they're being pushed. This can bore buyers, make them less likely to feel affection toward you, shut them down, and put them on the defensive. If you're doing all the talking, they'll feel like you are self-centered, don't care about them, and don't understand their situations and needs (even if you do). Worst of all, savvy buyers will peg you as an amateur and dismiss you.

Salespeople are often told, at some point in their careers, "The salespeople who succeed the most always ask great questions." This is true to a point; asking incisive questions is critical to sales success, but some salespeople take the advice too literally. They always ask questions, don't share a point of view or an opinion, don't tell stories, and don't help set the agenda for success. Buyers get bored with this quickly as well, and feel like they're getting the third degree. Although questions can be quite valuable, buyers can feel they are missing out on the full value they should get from you if you just ask question after question. The key is to balance advocacy and inquiry and to learn when to use one or the other.

IN is Influence: In Chapter 11 we discuss the 16 Principles of Influence, which you can apply throughout your sales conversations. Master these principles and you'll become more effective in each stage of your rainmaking conversations.

Robust as it is, the power of the RAIN model is that while, like anything, the more you practice the better you'll become, you can apply it right away and have it make a difference. Just remember what RAIN stands for, and you'll be well on your way. Although elegant models have deep intrinsic value, they are also easy to understand and apply.

In *Rainmaking Conversations,* we outline concepts and give examples of each component of RAIN. Once you are comfortable with what happens at each stage, you will be ready to lead masterful rainmaking conversations. Although these conversations come in many shapes and sizes, there are essentially six types of rainmaking conversations you'll need to be able to lead:

1. *Conversations with anybody* . . . where you begin new relationships, enhance current ones, and answer questions like, "What do you do?" Do this well at business events like conferences, seminars, and at personal events like the kids' soccer matches and family reunions, and you'll be able to turn these conversations into opportunities. Also, you'll help people know in what situations and to whom they should refer you. Succeeding here is the core subject of Chapter 4. Understanding and communicating your value proposition is essential for these initial introduction conversations, and it will serve you well in all types of rainmaking conversations.

2. *Prospecting conversations* . . . where you create a conversation that will eventually lead to a sale. Prospecting by telephone is the subject of Chapter 13.

3. *Core sales conversations* . . . where you lead each sales call, from the first sale to the close, with skill and confidence. You learn how to lead rainmaking conversations with RAIN Selling through the book, and you also get tips and examples of how to shepherd a great sales meeting in Chapter 16.

4. *Presentations and product demonstrations* . . . where you deliver key messages and content, share specifics about product and service capabilities, and deliver custom-crafted solutions to solve the needs of particular prospects. Entire books are dedicated to the art of presenting compelling presentations and delivering excellent product demonstrations. The concepts and frameworks you learn in the book will help tremendously with presentations and demos, and we provide tips and examples along the way.

5. *Winning the deal* . . . where you close the sale stage of the process, and open the customer stage. Closing is a much misunderstood and maligned concept in selling. In fact, some of the most recent consultative sales theories and popular books about closing have done sellers a great disservice, one that we aim to correct. We cover what you really need to know about closing in Chapter 15. And,

before you get to the top of the mountain, the last few steps often include difficult obstacles. Overcoming objections is the subject of Chapter 14.

6. *Account management and expansion* . . . where you work to service, resell, cross-sell, and up-sell your current clients. Although, as you can imagine, the dynamics of leading a conversation with a current customer is a little different and usually much easier than a sales call with a new prospect, the principles of RAIN will help you excel in account management and expansion.

> **Rainmaker:** Top performing salesperson. Rainmakers often outperform average sales reps by 300 percent to 500 percent.[4]

RASP—Four Keys to Rainmaking Success

Companies and individuals that achieve significantly higher sales results than the rest focus (whether they realize it or not) on four areas: Role Readiness, Action, Skills and Knowledge, and Process (RASP). This is what the best do. Unfortunately for those who seek to become top performers, too many well-known sales methods focus heavily on sales process and skills, but rarely on readiness, action, or knowledge.

This is both sad and unfortunate (well, sad and unfortunate to everyone else, not you, because you're about to learn a better way), and it's also backward. Here's why:

> **Role Readiness:** The degree to which a person is *fundamentally* prepared to succeed in sales.
> **Action:** The execution of activities that will lead to sales.

---

[4] According to the U.S. Bureau of Labor Statistics in 2009, the top 10 percent of wage earners in sales made 295 percent more than the median, www.bls.gov/oes/2009/may/oes410000.htm. Having analyzed the numbers ourselves from many organizations across industries, we've seen this to be largely accurate (depending on obvious factors like compensation structure), with the top sales reps earning much more.

> **Skills and Knowledge:** Skills—the various abilities needed to sell, and the degree to which a person can perform them well. Knowledge—the grasp of information needed for selling, and the ability to discuss relevant information and topics fluently.
>
> **Process:** A system or framework in which to perform actions to achieve the best possible sales results.

Role Readiness

We once had the "pleasure" of working regularly with a middle manager who had a bad attitude. How bad? Let's call him Darth. He was defensive, purposefully vague, withheld information, tore people down to build himself up, spent more time sneering at colleagues than collaborating with them, and wielded a red light saber. Every once in a while, however, the Emperor, Darth's boss, whom Darth respected deeply, would coach him to drop the bad attitude and actually help his colleagues.

For two weeks at a time, he would! He'd make his intentions clear, smile, build rapport in meetings, throw no one under the TIE fighter, and fulfill the commitments he made to others.

After two weeks . . . good-bye Anakin and welcome back Darth.

The moral of the story: Just because someone has the skills and knowledge to be able to do something doesn't mean that that person will do it. Attitude and intent trump skills every day. This happens in sales perhaps more than any other area we've ever encountered.

> Watch your thoughts, for they become words.
> Watch your words, for they become actions.
> Watch your actions, for they become habits.
> Watch your habits, for they become character.
> Watch your character, for it becomes your destiny.
>
> —Anonymous

Many sales-training programs focus on sales process and sales skills, but they rarely focus on assessing and enhancing the drivers of sales success, or minimizing defractors that prevent success. These crucial elements and hidden weaknesses tremendously affect salespeople's abilities to have success in their conversations. If you want to succeed, you have to be ready.

- Chapter 2 helps you understand and adopt the mind-set that propels rainmakers to success.
- Chapter 11 helps you understand the principles of influence so you can apply them in your rainmaking conversations.
- Chapter 16 helps you succeed by sharing with you the knowledge that rainmakers employ in their sales conversations; the more of this knowledge you have, the more confident you'll be when speaking with customers and prospects.
- Chapter 17 helps you be ready and prepared to succeed in every call.
- Chapter 18 helps you see how common mistakes and hidden weaknesses derail sales conversations, and helps you avoid making them yourself.

Action

We've seen more people *intend* to become top performers in sales than those that actually do it.

Assume for a minute that someone is ready to succeed in sales, has the skills and knowledge, and has a great selling process . . . and then she goes on vacation for six months. Not much selling happens.

Action in sales is a simple concept: You succeed if you do the right amount of the right things effectively.

- *The right amount.* Most salespeople can get more done every day by setting overall goals, setting activity targets, and pushing themselves to find ways to get more done. Rigorous action planning and strong processes help immensely here.
- *The right things.* Always ask yourself, "Am I doing the things right now that will help me achieve my goals fastest?" If you're not, then you're probably not doing the right things. At a recent RAIN Group webinar, we polled the attendees, asking, "Do the people in your

company in selling roles know what they should be doing to achieve what they could achieve in sales?" Ninety-seven percent of the respondents said no.

Imagine what would happen if you had 100 sellers at your company and 97 percent of their colleagues said yes to the same question. Chapter 3 provides a framework and guidelines for you to set goals, put action plans in place, and execute the right amount of the right actions.

- *Effectively.* It's common to find that prospecting—filling the front end of the pipeline—is the most important action for a salesperson. Let's say you're making a huge amount (right amount) of calls to the right people (right things), and getting nowhere. If you don't have the skills and knowledge to get the outputs you need from the actions you take, then your actions are worthless.

Creating a rainmaking conversation takes action. Leading a rainmaking conversation takes action. Converting a conversation into a sale . . . you get the idea. We wrote *Rainmaking Conversations* with action always in mind. Each chapter will offer you ideas for what you can do to succeed. In particular, Chapter 3 and the accompanying resources available to you on www .raingroup.com/booktools will help you set the right goals to build the right road map for taking action.

On Titles, Roles, and Gender

Throughout this book we use the term *salespeople* to refer to people who are expected to bring in new business or increase business from existing accounts. Salesperson, business developer, consultant, accountant, engineer, lawyer, technologist, solution provider, practice leader, vice president, entrepreneur . . . whatever your title or function, if you want to learn how to create and lead masterful sales conversations, this book is for you. And, in it, we refer to you as *salesperson*. We know that's probably not your title.

We use the terms *client* and *customer* interchangeably because the concepts in the book apply universally. *Client* is often a term used in large account sales and in service organizations. The term *customer* is

(continued)

used as well in these situations and is universally understood. Some organizations prefer to use one term or the other. There's no change in meaning or connotation when we use one or the other.

Last, as readers, none of us is a fan of the construct "he or she" and its various permutations. Thus, we don't use it, but we don't want to come off as chauvinists either. Sometimes buyers and sellers are "she" and sometimes "he." We didn't even count which one we used more often.

Skills and Knowledge

You can't take action effectively if you don't have the skills and knowledge to do so. Throughout the course of this book we help you develop the skills, and understand the knowledge you need, so you can lead masterful rain-making conversations and succeed in sales overall.

Process

A process is a systematic approach to something. Systematic approaches have a number of benefits. They:

- Help you know where to start, where you are, and where you're heading next.
- Allow you to ask (and answer) questions like, "Am I doing the right things to get to the next step? Am I doing something that helps me get to the next step at all?" and, "How can I get to the next step more quickly and easily?"
- Provide a framework for a large number of people to undertake similar actions toward similar goals.
- Allow for measurement and continuous improvement.

This book focuses on the sales conversations, so we concern ourselves mostly with the processes of creating and leading them. For this, the RAIN model is our guide.

But, like baseball, it wouldn't make sense for us to throw you on the field without any preparation and expect you to play like a pro when you get there. There are things you need to attend to *before* you get there so you can knock it out of the park when you do.

Rainmaking Conversations follows a process, beginning with helping you take stock of your Readiness to succeed in a sales role, planning your Actions, helping you build Skills and Knowledge, and (of course, with RAIN) providing a Process for your rainmaking conversations.

The *Rainmaking Conversations* road map is outlined in Figure 1.2. As we cover the various topics in the book we'll let you know where we are on the road map.

10 Rainmaker Principles

We developed the RAIN Selling method to provide a framework, road map, and learning process for those who want to become rainmakers. Follow the *Rainmaking Conversations* road map and it will help you to sell effectively. But if you really want to achieve and join the ranks of the rainmaker elite, you should take the 10 Rainmaker Principles to heart.

After years of primary research in selling, in analyzing the body of research available in the field of sales, in observing the best sales professionals in action, in studying what the best companies do to create cultures of rainmaking success, and in working with salespeople to dramatically increase their production, we've found that the top rainmakers share 10 common principles.

1. *Play to win-win.* Rainmakers respect, and always try to satisfy, the best interests of prospects and clients as well as their own (the win–win part). They are also extremely dedicated to becoming top performers (the play-to-win part), exhibiting the hustle, passion, and intensity it takes to achieve what only the elite achieve.
2. *Live by goals.* Rainmakers are goal-setting and goal-following fanatics. Goals are a part of their daily rituals.
3. *Take action.* Rainmakers realize that goals without actions don't get you very far. While other people intend to take action and do more, rainmakers do it.

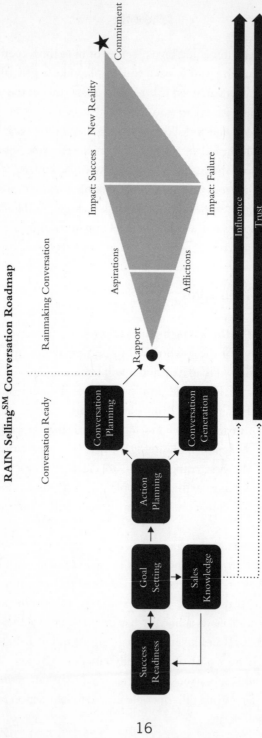

RAIN Selling^{SM} Conversation Roadmap

Conversation Ready   Rainmaking Conversation

Success Readiness — Goal Setting — Sales Knowledge — Action Planning — Conversation Planning — Conversation Generation

Rapport

Aspirations   New Reality

Afflictions   Commitment

Impact: Success

Impact: Failure

Influence

Trust

Figure 1.2 *Rainmaking Conversations* **Road Map**

4. *Think buying first, selling second.* Rainmakers map their selling processes to the processes and psychology of buying.
5. *Be a fluent expert.* Rainmakers are masters of market knowledge, customer needs, their products and services, their value, their competition, and everything else they need to know to succeed at selling. Rainmakers might not be technical experts in every area, but they know what they need to know to sell.
6. *Create new conversations every day.* Rainmakers always feed the front of their pipelines and improve their pipeline quality. They never coast, and rarely a day goes by when they don't speak to customers, prospects, and referral sources with the intent to source new business.
7. *Lead masterful rainmaking conversations.* Rainmakers lead masterful sales conversations, from prospecting to needs discovery to closing to account management.
8. *Set the agenda; be a change agent.* Rainmakers recommend, advise, and assist. They are change agents who are not afraid to push when it's in the best interest of the customer.
9. *Be brave.* It takes courage to rise to the occasion in sales. Rainmakers not only conquer their fears, they seek actively to win the most fruitful sales opportunities no matter how difficult the challenges may be.
10. *Assess yourself, get feedback, and improve continuously.* Rainmakers are never afraid to learn the cold, hard truth about themselves. They take what they discover—the good and the bad—to learn, grow, and change for the better. They never stop this cycle.

These 10 Rainmaker Principles form the core of the rainmaker's modus operandi. As you can see, they dovetail well with RASP and RAIN.

We point out regularly where specific content in *Rainmaking Conversations* relates to the 10 Rainmaker Principles. We also suggest that you take the 10 Rainmaker Principles[5] and post them on the wall in your workspace in an area where you can see them and read them once each day. Read them every day and they'll affect how you think. How you think will affect how you act. And how you act . . . well, that's the key to reaching your rainmaking destiny. Here's to the beginning of your long and fruitful journey down that path.

---

[5] Visit www.rainsalestraining.com/booktools to download a printable copy of the 10 Rainmaker Principles or to get a laminated copy of them sent to you.

They say the journey of a thousand miles begins with the first step. Indeed, the path to mastering rainmaking conversations begins with the first one, and it's the most important rainmaking conversation you'll ever have.

Let's start that conversation and see where it goes.

2

The Most Important Conversation You'll Ever Have

If you don't change your beliefs, your life will be like this forever. Is that good news?

—W. Somerset Maugham

A long time ago, a young Navajo boy was brooding over his poor performance in his first hunt with the young men of the tribe. The brooding lasted through the night and into the next day, when his father, seeing his son sulking, sat down with him. The father said, "Inside of us all there are two wolves. From the time we are born until the time we move on from this life, they battle. One wolf is Evil. It is regret, sorrow, greed, hate, inferiority, procrastination, false pride, misery, deceit, hubris, self-pity, guilt, anger, and bitterness. The other is Good. It is love, joy, kindness, abundance, loyalty, courage, honor, politeness, optimism, unselfishness, compassion, empathy, warmth, harmony, and hope."

The young boy went away and thought about his father's words. Later, he came back and asked, "Father, which wolf wins?"

His father replied, "The one you feed."

This is an old story, but it is told anew every day in sales.

In sales, the good wolf is desire, goals, commitment, action, bravery, positive attitude, energy, and responsibility for success. The evil wolf is indecision, lack of commitment, fear of rejection, aimlessness, negativity, procrastination, blame, and hidden weakness.

The idea, as the boy's father says, is to feed the good wolf and starve the evil one.

Before you determine the feeding habits of your inner wolf, you must first evaluate its overall condition. As Rainmaker Principle 10 states, you need to assess yourself, get feedback, and improve continuously. Before you start on your path to improvement, the first question you need to ask yourself is, "What should I improve?"

This is the beginning of your most important rainmaking conversation: The one you have with yourself. This internal conversation has many parallels to those you'll have with prospects and clients. You'll discover your own needs by asking the right questions,[1] asking them in a way that gets to the heart of the answers, taking stock of the impact of various courses of action, and then setting the agenda for building a new and better reality. Only this time, you'll be selling to yourself.

Six Questions to Ask Yourself

To start the conversation about your quest to become a rainmaker, ask yourself the following six questions.

1. *How strong is my desire to achieve in sales?* The most important factor influencing whether or not you become a rainmaker is your personal desire

---

[1] Dave Kurlan has conducted extensive research into the drivers of sales success. At the time of this book's writing, Kurlan's company, Objective Management Group, and its partners (including us at RAIN Group) have conducted more than 500,000 assessments of salespeople and managers at more than 8,500 organizations. This research has informed the content in this chapter.

for success in sales. Note the emphasis on *in sales*. You might think for full-time salespeople this goes without saying. It doesn't. Some salespeople can't wait to sell; others are just biding their time until something better comes along. The same is true of professional service providers. Many professionals have a tremendous desire to achieve in general, but not so much in sales (or, as it's more commonly referred to, business development). Some service providers don't think they're cut out for selling. Some are uncomfortable with learning to sell. Some are not money-motivated, and their companies don't reward them if they sell anyway. Some, however, love selling and, like children waiting to open birthday presents, they can't wait to get to it. *Why* they desire to sell is mostly immaterial—*that* they want to sell is essential.

> The best rainmakers are just those that are most passionate about what they do. They believe more than everyone else that what they do matters, and they're good at, and not shy about, articulating that.
>
> —Mike Sheehan, CEO, Hill Holliday

2. *How committed am I to doing what I need to do to succeed?* The premise of David Maister's book *Strategy and the Fat Smoker* is that people know what they need to do to help their companies and themselves succeed—they just don't do it. Maister compares the practice of management to the challenge of weight loss. How do you lose weight? Eat less and exercise more. Everyone knows it. Doing it is another story.

Salespeople often know what they need to do—make more phone calls, lead more rainmaking conversations, deepen relationships, become experts in their fields, learn new skills, go the extra mile for customers.

Although you might desire to succeed in sales, without the requisite commitment, you'll get the same results as you would if you wanted to lose weight, but then ordered a bucket of wings and hit the couch. For sure, most people who want to lose weight don't plan to do this, but it happens. It's 10 PM and you have been good all day. Then you break down and start winging it.

Commitment is tested when the going gets tough, and the tough eat salad. The going gets tough all the time in sales. It's not easy to create new conversations every day (Rainmaker Principle 6), live by goals (Rainmaker

Principle 2), ask the tough questions, take a risk, hold true to your value without caving on price, go the extra mile for the client . . . none of these is easy to do when faced with the distractions that crop up.

Desire to sell is the first step. Committing to action and taking it—that's the game-changing leap.

3. *How energetically will I pursue success?* You'll hear a lot of advice about how to work smarter. You can always work smarter, but working harder makes a big difference, too. Rainmaking conversations require a lot of work—you have to arrange the conversations, prepare rigorously, allot the time to conduct the conversation, and typically make multiple follow-up calls to close the deal.[2] Success with rainmaking conversations is a function of how many you have and how well you conduct them. Rainmakers create new conversations every day (Rainmaker Principle 6), lead masterful rainmaking conversations (Rainmaker Principle 7), and always improve their pipeline quality. Living by these principles takes time and energy.

4. *How's my attitude?* It's not our goal here to recount the benefits or rewrite the argument in favor of a positive attitude. We're here to help you succeed at selling, and, more specifically, succeed with sales conversations. We've encountered many salespeople who have the desire and the commitment to do what they should do to succeed, and then proceed to derail themselves with thoughts of doom and gloom about the economy, lack of faith in their company's products and services, and worries about their ability to lead successful sales conversations.

Along with the typical digs on the economy, their companies, and their products, the doom-and-gloomers say things like, "I don't like making phone calls to people I don't know well," "CEOs aren't my peers and I am uncomfortable speaking with them," and "I'm not good at building rapport and developing new relationships quickly."

They say these words and, like magic, the words become true. Go into a sales conversation with negative thoughts, and even if you think you have built the best dam to keep these thoughts out, they'll find the holes and flood

---

[2] 38.6 percent of sales take 3 to 5 calls to close, 30.9 percent take 6 to 9 calls, 12 percent take 10 to 15 calls, and 6.9 percent take more than 15 calls. CSO Research, "Sell Cycle Review Analysis," 2010.

your mind with doubt. Once your mind is flooded with doubt, the flood can't help but leak into your sales conversations.

Sales is a game of opportunity. If you think the opportunity can't, won't, or shouldn't happen for you, it won't. But if you think it can, will, and should happen to you, when opportunity knocks you'll be ready to welcome it in for coffee and dessert.

> Those who are fired with an enthusiastic idea and who allow it to take hold and dominate their thoughts find that new worlds open for them. As long as enthusiasm holds out, so will new opportunities.
>
> —Norman Vincent Peale, *The Power of Positive Thinking* (1952)

5. *Do I accept responsibility for my outcomes, or do I make excuses?* There's always a good reason for why we don't do something we mean to do, don't reach the goal we set for ourselves, or don't reach our potential. When this happens, do you blame circumstances or other people, or do you take responsibility?

Some people succeed despite adversity. They beat a bad economy, they create conversations with difficult-to-reach decision makers, they sell something complex and intangible to someone who never even had an inkling that they wanted to buy it until the salesperson came knocking. Yet at the same company, selling the same products and services to the same market, other people tell us, "I can't hit my goals in this economy," "The decision makers are just too insulated to get to," and "I can't sell something they don't want."

The excuse makers always have good reasons why they didn't prospect, didn't prepare well for a meeting, and didn't make those last few follow-up calls before they left the office for the day. One salesperson we were coaching told us that after working to set goals and build a sales action plan, he didn't implement the plan because he didn't have a system that met with his satisfaction for updating his progress. (Sure, technology can always help, but in his situation a notebook and a pen would have worked just fine.)

We all have the same amount of time each day, the same number of days each week, and the same power to make decisions concerning what we choose to do and not do.

There's no one keeping you from getting it done but yourself.

6. *Am I willing to face my sales demons?* On September 9, 1965, James Stockdale, a pilot in the United States Navy, ejected from his A-4E Skyhawk, descended into a small village in North Vietnam, and was taken prisoner. He spent much of the next eight years, from then until his release on February 12, 1973, in a 3- by 9-foot cell with the light on 24 hours a day.

Despite great hardship, Stockdale persevered. He went on to a storied career in the navy (president of the Naval War College) and in education (president of the Citadel, fellow at the Hoover Institution at Stanford University). As told in Jim Collins' book *Good to Great*, he recounted how he always kept the faith, but was willing to confront the hard, brutal truth of his situation, never willing to sugarcoat or lie to himself that things were better than they were.

If you've been honest with yourself after asking the first five questions you might be thinking, "I know some areas in which I can improve." You can stop here, or you can keep looking to find the rest of the hard, brutal truth. Many will stop here, but rainmakers look at one more area: their hidden weaknesses.

Hidden weaknesses aren't as obvious as desire, commitment, attitude, and the rest. They include nonsupportive buy cycle, money discomfort, self-limiting record collection, need for approval, and tendency to become emotionally involved. If you're not familiar with these terms, you'll learn more about them and how they regularly derail sales conversations later in Chapter 18.

Outcomes from Your Conversation with Yourself

Great conversations lead to choices. After you have your conversation with yourself, you'll have a few decisions to make. In each area, you have Option 1 and Option 2. Think long and hard. Which wolf will you feed?

Topic	Option 1	Option 2
Desire	Want more success	Happy with how things are
Commitment	Will do whatever it takes	Will do it if it's not that difficult
Energy	Ready to put the time and effort in	Other things take precedence
Attitude	The world is my oyster	Obstacles are too great to overcome
Responsibility	I'm responsible for my success and my team's success	My success is not in my control
Hidden weaknesses	I want to know what they are for me because I want them gone	Better to leave well enough alone

Regardless of what your answers are, the first thing you have to know is, "Am I willing to look?" Assuming the answer is yes, and you'd like to explore further, visit www.rainsalestraining.com/booktools for more insight.

3 | Goal and Action Planning

Making the Most Rain

I get up every morning determined to both change the world and have one hell of a good time. Sometimes this makes planning my day difficult.

—E.B. White

Avoiding what we know we should be doing. Doing something other than what we should be doing. Justifying our inaction. There's something confounding about our capacity as human beings to know we should be doing one thing and then avoid it like a peanut butter and tuna fish sandwich.

In our personal lives, we know we should clean the garage, call our dad to say hello, and exercise at least three times this week.

But we don't.

In our sales efforts, we know we should make five more calls before the day is through, organize our contact list and our follow-up process to become more efficient, and invite that client out to dinner.

But we don't.

Procrastination wins all too often. Worst of all, we know that by doing the sales activities we should do, we will achieve much greater financial and career success than we have now. The benefits are real and tangible. But we still don't. There are a million ~~excuses~~ reasons we give ourselves to justify why we can't do what we should. Here are a few favorites:

- Don't have the time right now.
- Have other things I need to do first.
- Can get to it tomorrow.
- Was derailed by other people's requests and agendas.
- Need some balance in life so I am going home now.
- Not certain this is the right thing to do.
- Doubt whether I will succeed at this.
- Don't like doing this so ended up doing something else.
- Not sure why I didn't do it, just didn't.
- Too tired.
- It's too difficult to do.
- Other people might see me fail . . . I might see me fail . . . I'll fail so why start . . . fail fail fail.

The list goes on, but the theme is the same: Something gets in the way of our doing what we should and want to do. The conversation with ourselves doesn't go well.

Fortunately, we're all in control of our own sales destinies. It might not feel like it sometimes because the road to success is always under repair, but it's true. Everything on the earlier list—and everything else you can think of—is just a pothole on the road to success if you choose to approach it that way. You can either get stuck in the potholes, or you can navigate around, over, and through them on your way to achievement, financial freedom, recognition, or whatever it is that motivates you.

> The road to success is always under repair.

If you want to succeed with rainmaking conversations (and you probably do since you're reading this book), you have to generate conversations every day (Rainmaker Principle 6) and have the skills to lead them well (Rainmaker Principle 7). These two goals are worthy in and of themselves, but they are not lone islands. They should be a part of a larger set of sales goals, a goal archipelago, so to speak, that will get you to the ultimate career and life destinations you seek.

As you read the rest of this chapter, we help you to continue the conversation you have with yourself by developing a set of goals to get you to that destination.

Why Goals Are Important

The key to leaving the excuses behind and to achieving what you want and know you can achieve is living by goals (Rainmaker Principle 2).

There are a million and one stories about how a person, family, department, or company has been stuck in one pothole or another. One of our personal favorites is IBM. As recounted in *Who Says Elephants Can't Dance?*,[1] when Lou Gerstner took over in April, 1993, IBM was dangerously close to running out of cash. The company was stuck in an enormous pothole. Although the story of what he did to turn around the organization has many facets, one central theme stands out: Gerstner set goals and commitments for the organization, aligned them throughout,[2] and stopped at nothing to execute them. He led the company from the brink of disaster to a resounding success within a few years.

Tim King, founder of Urban Prep High School in Chicago, faced a drastically different—but equally daunting—task. He had a vision to take 150 of the poorest, most disadvantaged boys out of the failing public school system and enroll them in Urban Prep, a new charter school he developed dedicated to one goal: 100 percent of the graduating class would go to college four years later.

He faced challenging odds:

- Fewer than 50 percent of black male students who enter high school in Chicago graduate.
- Only one in five goes on to college after graduation.
- Of the 150 students enrolled at Urban Prep:
  — Four percent were reading at or above grade level.
  — Eighty percent were from low income families.
  — The great majority were from single parent homes.

---

[1] Louis V. Gerstner, *Who Says Elephants Can't Dance?* (New York: HarperCollins, 2002).
[2] Indeed, every employee would make three "personal business commitments," or actions to fulfill broader IBM commitments. Performance against those commitments was directly tied to salary. www.forbes.com/2002/11/11/cx_ld_1112gerstner.html.

Tim King's story about what he did to get 100 percent of graduating students heading off to college (to schools that include Trinity College, University of Illinois, Howard University, University of Virginia, Morehouse College, Georgetown, and Tuskegee) is both fascinating and instructive, but one thing is clear: King lived by his goal. As he said, "I wanted to create a school that was going to put black boys in a different place, and in my mind, that different place needed to be college."

King then set the goal: 100 percent of the students that graduate would head off to college the next year. Four years later, the 95 who graduated all did.

Much has been written about the power of setting goals, regularly reviewing them, and managing your time and activities to achieve them. In one 30-year tracking study by John Hunter and Robert Rogers, managers who were committed to goals and objectives in their management processes showed an average increase of 56 percent in the productivity of their operations. Of those who had goals but weren't committed to doing what they needed to do to reach them, the average increase in productivity was only 6 percent. In the same study, they also completed an analysis of 70 other research studies, 68 of which showed productivity gains when managers crafted and managed to goals and objectives.[3]

Do Rainmakers Have Written Goals?

A review of assessment results of 400,000 salespeople compared the top 5 percent versus the bottom 5 percent.[4] Among the results was the following:

- Top 5 percent of salespeople: 100 percent have written goals.
- Bottom 5 percent of salespeople: 16 percent have written goals.

We could continue to make the case for pages and pages, and cite example after example, about the power of goals and action plans. We'll resist that temptation starting now and leave it at this: Those who reach rainmaker status

---

[3] John E. Hunter and Robert Rodgers, "Impact of Management by Objectives on Organizational Productivity," *Journal of Applied Psychology*. ISSN: 0021-9010. 1991.

[4] www.omghub.com/salesdevelopmentblog/tabid/5809/bid/11304/Ultimate-Comparison-of-Top-Salespeople-versus-Salespeople-That-Fail.aspx.

don't get there by accident—they live by goals (Rainmaker Principle 2), and they are committed to doing what they need to do to achieve.

Living by Goals

Over the years we've seen many salespeople (and sales managers and companies) get goal planning, action planning, and commitment right, and we've seen many fall short.

Two things set apart those who live by their goals and those who don't:

1. They know where they're headed.
2. They commit to a goals routine.

First, people who have goals know where they want to go. You might be thinking, "I wish it were that simple . . . I have no idea what I want to do when I grow up, and never have." It's not our purpose here, in a book about rainmaking conversations, to guide you in discovering your inner purpose.

But contrary to what you might read in others' writings about goals, you don't have to sort out your life's purpose in order to achieve success in sales. Start by setting a target. It can be as simple as having an annual sales quota, and having the answer to the question, "Do I really want to achieve this badly?" be yes.

Second, once you know where you want to go, commit to a goals routine.

Keeping your goals routine simple will help you stick to it. Here's a simple road map we've created that can help you build and stick to your own goals routine:

- Review your goals first thing in the morning every day. Say your big picture goal out loud (yes, seriously[5]), then scan your plan for the

---

[5] Affirmations are well documented to enhance goal achievement. For example, at Urban Prep (remember Tim King), every morning the students must recite, together, "We believe. We are college bound. We are exceptional—not because we say it, but because we work hard at it. We believe in ourselves. We believe."

week and review goals and actions for the day. This should take a few minutes. At the end of each day, review how the day went, and set goals and actions for the next day.

- On Friday or during the weekend, review the week and set goals and actions for the next week. Once per week (this can be at your Friday or weekend review session), review your goals with a goals partner. Your goals partner can be a peer, a mentor, a coach, or a friend, but it's someone you work with explicitly each week to make sure you're on top of your goals, staying committed, and pushing yourself. Along with goals, milestones, and progress, you should discuss any hassles or potholes holding you back so you can fight your way through them.

- Once per month, meet with a small group of people you trust to review what you're doing, where you're headed, what you'll do in the next month, and get ideas for how you can achieve more and shake off any nagging hassles.

- Once per quarter, review your progress toward your annual goal. During this meeting step back and ask yourself, "What do I absolutely, positively need to get done over the next three months to achieve my annual goals?" Set no more than three priorities for the next quarter that you'll direct all your passion, energy, and intensity toward so you can stay on track to meet your annual target.

- Once per year, set your targets for the next year. Make sure you ask yourself, "What do I need to do to get to my big-picture goal?" When you're done with your goals and annual plan, ask yourself, "If I get done what I am about to do, will it help me get to my big-picture goal?" Make sure it does before you put your head down for a year to make it happen.

- As you're crafting your goals, you should also take your big-picture goal (e.g., becoming the top-performing salesperson in the company five years in a row, making $500,000 a year, getting promoted to senior vice president, owning the Milwaukee Bucks, retiring at 45) and align it to shorter-term goals and actions. If you don't see that connection, you will fall victim to excuses and distractions along the way.

Sometimes when we're working with people to craft their goals and actions they get hung up on having "the right template" or detailed tracking mechanism, and because they don't have it, they don't even get started.

Don't let this happen to you.

Some of the best goal setters we know write their goals on one sheet of paper and stick it in the top drawer of their desk. (And, no, they're not all 90 years old.) One person we have worked with for years keeps a Word file on his desktop, and reopens the document each week to review and update progress.

Sales Goals Questions to Answer

1. What's my big-picture, long-term goal? (Just one big one.)
2. What's my three- to five-year goal? (Can be more than one, but no more than three.)
3. What are my personal income and financial goals?
4. What is my sales goal for the next 12 months? What are the Critical Success Factors I need to commit to in order to achieve the sales goal? (No more than five.)
5. What are the success metrics I must achieve throughout the year, each quarter, and each month to reach my goals?
6. What are the short-term goals I must achieve and the actions I must undertake this week (or month) to reach my annual target?
7. What's my plan for today?

It's true: The road to success is always under repair. Live by goals and you won't get lost on the side streets, wondering to yourself why you're not there yet.

Once you have your goals set, you'll need to outline a set of specific activities to help you achieve them. Visit www.rainsalestraining.com/booktools for a list of 39 planning questions, and a set of tools to help you build an action plan for yourself.

4

Understanding and Communicating Your Value Proposition

Complex problems have simple, easy to understand, wrong answers.

—H. L. Mencken

Let's say you've worked with a customer for two years and you have a great relationship. If we called this customer and asked, "Why do you work with, and keep working with, XYZ and Company?" What would they say?

Because we've asked this question so many times when doing research for RAIN Group clients, we expect we'd get long, glowing stories of business impact realized, trust, positive work relationships, respect for our client as a leader in their area, and more.

Now, let's say you've been working with a prospect for a number of months on a major sale. If you've followed the RAIN Selling method, you have a clear idea of the impact you can have on the client and what their new reality will be like after they buy from you. They probably do, too.

It's not like either of these situations when you *first* meet someone. The person doesn't know you, what you do, or what you've done. *When you first meet someone,* positioning the great value that you provide and impact you can have isn't easy. Communicating value when you first meet someone is one of the greatest problems that all salespeople have. They tell us:

- Our products and services are difficult to describe—it's impossible to pare down all that we do into a brief statement.
- Our solutions are customized to each client's particular need, so it's impossible to encapsulate.
- We help our customers in a broad range of areas so it's difficult to know what will resonate because we could talk about so many things.
- It's easy to talk about the specifics of what we do, but difficult to quantify the impact.
- Our products and services are commodities (or our customers perceive them to be). There's no real "value" over what other companies can do.
- I always feel so contrived and uncomfortable delivering an elevator pitch. . . . I never feel like it comes across the way it should.

Whatever you sell, if you can't describe it and the value it offers, you'll always have trouble getting buyers to buy it. The ability to position your value in a way that grabs attention and communicates the benefits of working with you, and does so in a way that naturally leads into the rest of the conversation, is vital to your ability to lead rainmaking conversations.

A Value Proposition Is Not a Statement

Let's say someone asks you the simple question, "What do you do?" Although you might need to include value in your answer, take note: A value proposition is, in itself, not a statement.

A *value proposition* is the collection of reasons why someone buys. This, at least, is our definition. Not everyone agrees.

From Investopedia:[1]

---

[1] www.investopedia.com/terms/v/valueproposition.asp

What Does *Value Proposition* Mean? A business or marketing statement that summarizes why a consumer should buy a product or use a service. This statement should convince a potential consumer that one particular product or service will add more value or better solve a problem than other similar offerings.

Companies use this statement to target customers who will benefit most from using the company's products, and this helps maintain an economic moat. The ideal value proposition is concise and appeals to the customer's strongest decision-making drivers. Companies pay a high price when customers lose sight of the company's value proposition.

You'll note the Investopedia definition characterizes a value proposition as a statement. Trying to boil the concept of value down to a statement is a simple, easy-to-understand, misguided approach.

If you think of a value proposition not as a statement, but as the aggregate sum of the factors that get people to buy, then you have much more with which to work. It's from that concept—the collection of reasons why people buy from you—that you can put your selling efforts to work much more effectively, communicating different components of that value in different ways for different situations.

One of these situations is, indeed, to describe your value in broad strokes when you introduce yourself and your company. This is when you can use a value proposition *positioning* statement.

A *value proposition positioning statement* is a compelling, tangible statement of how a company or individual will benefit from buying from you.

You take parts of your overall value proposition and craft key points into a statement. This way a prospect can get the overall sense of how you can help, and get that sense quickly.

For example, we at RAIN Group help companies to improve their sales performance. If you want your salespeople, professionals, and leaders to sell more, we can help.

This is the umbrella under which we operate. The purpose is to help our clients and prospects wrap their heads around the general area where we help, and to know when they should work with us.

A *value proposition* is the collection of reasons why someone buys. A *value proposition positioning statement* is a compelling, tangible statement of how a company or individual will benefit from buying from you.

Ultimately, this is why our clients buy from RAIN Group—because we help them increase sales. But there is always a set of underlying factors and specifics that sway them to choose us versus doing something themselves, choosing someone else to help them, or choosing to do nothing at all.

Too many salespeople only craft and practice a statement. They don't investigate the various underlying components of why buyers buy from them. If you think of a value proposition as only a statement, you'll stop here, too. If you truly understand the collection of reasons why buyers value what you sell, then you can have much richer and more persuasive conversations.

Three Legs of the Value Proposition Stool

The collection of reasons why people buy fall into three major buckets:

1. Prospects have to want and need what you're selling. You have to *resonate*.
2. Potential buyers have to see why you stand out from the other available options. You have to *differentiate*.
3. Potential buyers have to believe that you can deliver on your promises. You have to *substantiate*.

What happens if you don't attend to this holy value propositions trinity? Like a three-legged stool, if you take one leg away the entire stool topples over, illustrated in Figure 4.1:

- Remove resonance, and people won't be interested in what you're selling.

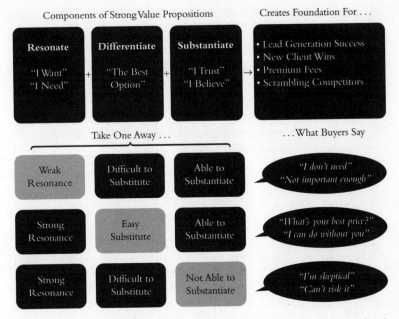

Figure 4.1 Three legs of the value proposition stool, and what happens when you remove a leg.

- Remove differentiation, and buyers will pressure you on price or attempt to get what you sell someplace else.
- Remove your ability to substantiate your claims, and although customers may want what you sell (you resonate), and may perceive that you stand out from the crowd (you differentiate), they don't believe you can produce what you say you can. Thus, they won't risk working with you or buying your product.

Before you come up with your value proposition positioning *statement*, focus first on understanding all of the components that make up the three legs of your value proposition stool. Only then can you communicate your value in your sales conversations. You can sum it all up in a short statement, too, but you'll be way ahead of your competitors who are satisfied with a canned statement only.

Six Common Mistakes When Describing What You Do

In addition to the major points outlined in this chapter, there are six other common mistakes salespeople make when describing what they do.

1. **No substance**

   We offer efficient and effective products and solutions to Fortune 500 and emerging growth companies, helping them to uncover and capitalize on known as well as hidden opportunities to provide value to their customers and increase shareholder value. We're unique because . . .

2. **Too long**

   It all started when I was five and read my first book on EPA compliance . . . by the time I was 13, I had capped my first brown field . . . then in the third year after starting the firm, we launched our emissions testing division. . . .

3. **Too short/cute/clever**

   - *We're the semiconductor company that wins.*
   - *We make our clients' financials sing.*
   - *We're the leading-with-integrity technology products company.*

4. **Laundry list**

   We are a law firm, and we focus on admiralty law, alternative dispute resolution, antitrust, bankruptcy, appellate litigation, complex litigation, debt financing, environmental law, foreign trade, government relations, ice cream patent and trademark, koala bear adoption. . . .

5. **Not prepared for the question**

   Well, um, you see in capital-intense businesses there sometimes is a situation where the capitalization structure needs to be re-engineered because . . . well, there's really a lot to it. Okay, from a big-picture perspective we tend to focus on smokestack businesses, but only where their capital structure . . .

6. **Scripted elevator pitch**

   Many salespeople write a tightly scripted elevator pitch that they practice over and over. When it comes time to use it, it comes out like a canned monologue, and it comes out the same way to every person, regardless of their perspective. It often falls flat, seems impersonal, and doesn't resonate because it doesn't consider the point of view of the receiver of the message.

Focus on Impact, Not Mechanics, to Break Free of the Commodity Trap

When you craft messages about what you do, think in terms of the customer needs you solve, not what products and services you offer. When you meet someone for the first time, your conversation partner will likely not yet know the details about your offerings, and it's not time to share them. You can, however, quickly position the aspirations you help companies achieve, the afflictions you help solve, and the impact of doing so.

When you tell people what you do by describing the tasks you perform, it will lead you down a less fruitful path than when you talk about the outcomes you can deliver.

Consider the following:

A man is walking by a construction site, and he comes upon somebody laying bricks and he asks the person, "What are you doing?" The worker looks at him and says, "I'm laying bricks."

The man continues walking down the road, and he comes to another worker doing the same thing and he says, "What are you doing?" And this worker says, "I'm building a wall."

He continues one more step down that building site, and he comes to a third worker laying bricks and he says, "What are you doing?" And the worker turns to him and says, "I'm building a cathedral."

Laying brick is a commodity. If you are viewed as selling a commodity, you won't stand out and you'll face constant price pressure.

Whatever your "cathedral" is creates visions in the minds of the buyer, starting you on the path of creating a new reality. Depending on what cathedral you're selling, by starting with the outcome, you'll likely elicit emotions from prospects. They'll think about the last time they tried to do whatever it is that you do. They might think, for example, how poorly it turned out, how upset they were when it failed, how they wish they could get it done well, and how they'd feel if it were successful.

Example: Impact versus Mechanics

We worked with a web-consulting firm that had, believe it or not, sent out 25 proposals and won zero. Clearly, they were doing something wrong. They were getting called to the table. They had a decent reputation, but they weren't closing the deal.

When we looked at their proposals and the way they talked about their solutions, we found that they were talking only about the technicalities and process of building web sites. They positioned themselves as a commodity.

Any of their prospects could leave the conversation, talk to two other providers, line them all up in a row and they'd all seem to "do" exactly the same technical work. Except that with our client they might be overwhelmed and turned off by all the technical talk.

We worked with the firm and asked them to try a different strategy, starting by asking them a series of questions:

- What's it like working with you?
- Forget the building blocks of how you get there, what are the deliverables?
- What is the impact that your clients receive at the end of working with you?
- What frustrations have your clients had when working with other firms?

That's when the web consultants realized that they don't just build web sites. They build all different types of company and marketing successes.

They started to articulate this value to prospects in their conversations and in their proposals. They went from going 0 for 25 on proposals, to two for two, generating six figures of revenue from the start.

The first step to getting out of the commodity trap is to stop thinking about yourself as a commodity. If you think of yourself as a commodity, that's how you'll come across. Stop talking about the mechanics of your offerings, and start talking about the impact and new reality.

Six Building Blocks of Value Proposition Positioning Statements

You recall from earlier that a *value proposition positioning statement* is a compelling, tangible statement of how a company or individual will benefit from buying from you.

You can use these statements to introduce yourself competently to another person, and begin a rainmaking conversation.

There are six building blocks you want to consider using in your value proposition positioning statement:

1. *Target customers.* Whom do you serve? What makes for an ideal customer regarding industry, location, size, type, and so on? This allows the person on the receiving end to think, "They work with companies like ours." Know your target customer so you can craft messages that will resonate with them. In addition, the more you can specialize the messeage for a particular buyer set, the more you differentiate.

2. *Need/business problem.* What types of needs and business problems do you address? How do you help? This helps prospects understand how and when they should use you.

3. *Impact of solving need.* What are the financial and emotional benefits of solving the need? How do you provide value? You may be thinking, "We do so much, and the specifics are always different." When crafting your value proposition positioning statement, choose one or two, generalize the type of impact, and later, in proof of concept, you can give a specific example or two. This helps people see why they should address the needs you can help them address.

4. *Your offerings.* What's your product and service approach, how do you run your company, solve problems, and work with customers? Notice that company and offerings are fourth here. Don't lead with your capabilities. Take a customer-centric approach and frame your offerings within the context of the needs you can help solve.

5. *Proof of concept.* How can you demonstrate that your approach has worked to solve similar problems for others? How do you substantiate your claims? How do they know that what you say will happen will actually happen?

Your ability to differentiate from the competition in your initial discussions will significantly increase your ability to get to the next step in the sales process. You are more than three times as likely to convert at least 75 percent of your discussions if you exceed buyers' expectations when it comes to differentiation.[2]

You can use reference stories and case studies to provide evidence for your customers to substantiate your claims.

6. *Distinction.* Why is your offering preferable to other options for solving the need? Do you have something unique about you that's worthwhile to share? Is there some way to highlight how you're different from others? This creates differentiation of your company versus others.

These six building blocks dovetail with the "resonate, differentiate, substantiate" concepts to help you develop messages you can use in sales conversations.

Be careful, though, not to create one canned statement that encapsulates each of these six positioning points that you use in every conversation. Remember, these are building blocks. Just like the wooden blocks we all had as kids, you can use the same blocks to build all sorts of different shapes, towers, and cathedrals. You pick and choose which blocks to use in your conversations based on the particular situation.

For example, say you're a marketing and brand consultant talking to your cousin Madison, who happens to be a private school teacher. She asks you to explain what you do in more detail after you mention that you are a consultant. You might say something like this:

In private schools, how do you think they get students to enroll? Generally families might look at and evaluate three to five schools before choosing one. But what do you think causes some schools to have thriving enrollment and long waitlists while others struggle to get new students? Large organizations have to ask themselves these same

---

[2] CSO Insights, "Sales Performance Optimization Report: Sell Cycle Review Analysis," 20.

questions—except rather than talking about student enrollment, they are talking about consumers buying their products. Why do you choose Colgate over Crest? I help large organizations answer these types of questions for their businesses. I just helped a company that sells dog toys reposition a product line and get it into a major department store chain that they've been trying to get into for four years. They tripled their sales.

If you were talking to a prospect you met at a networking event, the answer might sound something like this:

I help leaders of large packaged goods companies understand why consumers decide to buy one brand over another. For example, just last week I presented findings to a client where we uncovered X, Y, and Z. It's really interesting stuff that will likely lead to $20 million in new sales over the next three years if they implement our recommended changes. Our last client in a similar situation got $30 million, actually.

Same building blocks, but tailored for the person with whom you are speaking.

Figures 4.2 and 4.3 are a couple of real-world examples that put these building blocks in practice:

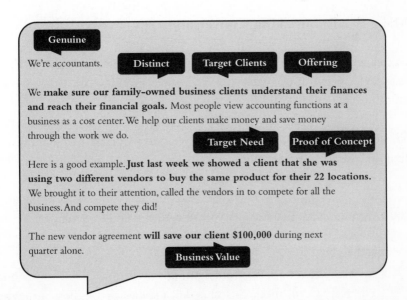

Figure 4.2

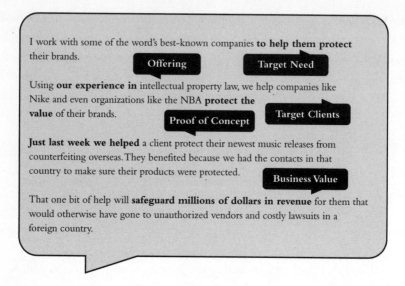

Figure 4.3

Once you have the proper building blocks on reserve, you'll be ready in any rainmaking conversation to properly position your value.

Make It a Rainmaking Conversation

Earlier we wrote, "We at RAIN Group help companies to improve their sales performance. If you want your salespeople, professionals, and leaders to sell more, we can help."

Did we follow our format? Yes, but we kept it short and general. After all, we don't know who *you* are or what *you* care about. We could, however, find this out in a conversation.

Rest assured we have:

- Various industries we have worked with closely. Depending on where we are, we are prepared to talk about our depth of experience in that industry.
- Specific needs we solve, from figuring out what will boost sales at one company versus another, closing skill and knowledge gaps, hiring the best salespeople, and others.

- Detailed knowledge of the impact of solving our clients' needs, from increasing results of each salesperson, to increasing new sales hire success, to speeding up new sales hire ramp-up time.

We have specific success stories in each area, quite a number of differentiators, a long client list, and a lot of research and intellectual capital behind our approaches.

If we were to deliver all these messages at once, however, not knowing our specific audience, we'd fall into the trap of giving a canned, one-size-fits-all value proposition positioning statement. (It would be too long, too.)

The point is this: If you know the value you offer and structure the conversation right, you can generate interest and desire subtly as you move along in a conversation. Do this, and you succeed in answering the question, "What do you do?" and position yourself and your value well in any discussion.

PART TWO

RAIN SELLING KEY CONCEPTS

5 | Rapport

The farmer, it appears, must not be approached too abruptly. If you are to get his money you must break the news to him gently. You should first talk about horses, soil, and market conditions. This conversation will show that you are interested in things close to him and likewise give you a chance to study his temperament and to learn his likes and dislikes, and discover his weaknesses.

—Clarence Darrow in *The American Mercury* in 1925 writing about the topic of "Salesmanship"

The concepts of rapport building and personal likeability are not new. You can find book after book written from the 1920s onward that will teach you techniques for building rapport. For example, you might be told to look around the potential buyer's office and talk about what you see. "Ah, I see you have a big fish on your wall. Are you a fishing enthusiast? I go trout fishing all the time in Wyoming. Let's talk about trout." Unfortunately, many people today, both buyers and sellers, equate the concept of rapport building with this type of contrived chitchat.

Rapport building is not the planned buttering up of the buyer before a salesperson moves in for the kill. The mind-set behind this approach to rapport building is underhanded and sneaky. Our emphatic response to this approach: Don't do it.

Yet the fundamental underlying need for a buyer to connect with a seller—or at least to generally like him or her—exists and must be attended to. At least, it must if you want to generate new business and grow your accounts.

In our research report *How Clients Buy,*[1] 26 percent of buyers surveyed reported that they have experienced having no personal chemistry with sellers in their last few buying situations. In and of itself this might not seem like a problem—although, who wants to feel that they have cultivated no personal connection with 26 out of 100 potential customers? But, we also learned that 85 percent of these same disconnected buyers would be either somewhat or much more likely to consider purchasing from that same salesperson if some kind of personal chemistry was established.

I Liked Them Better

One company where we both worked was going public. The process of selecting an accounting firm to help take us public included discussions with all five of what were, at the time, the Big Five accounting firms. When we ultimately selected one of them, I (Mike) asked our chief financial officer—the primary decision maker—why we chose one firm over the others.

We proceeded to the CFO's office where he showed me the detailed grid of the decision criteria and why this firm was the best. We talked about it for a few minutes and I was astounded. As a young leader in a fast-growing firm, I felt I had just learned a valuable skill in how senior leaders make important decisions. It was all very scientific and analytical.

Then he closed the door. "Do you want to hear the real reason I picked them?"

"Sure," I said.

He said, "I liked them best."

He went on to tell me that three out of the five firms had the experience and capability to do a competent job of taking us public. He could argue, even, that one of the firms we didn't select had a couple of advantages (though nothing too important) over the firm that we did select.

---

[1] Mike Schultz and John Doerr, *How Clients Buy* (RainToday, 2009).

Here is a real-life example of the familiar, "People buy with their hearts and justify with their heads." All things being equal, he picked the provider he liked. He's not the only buyer who does it. All other things being sort-of equal, he picked the people that made the best personal connection to him.

Building Real Rapport

When you look to build rapport, keep in mind that what you want to do is make a sincere emotional connection. As you work to do this, consider the following:

Be genuine. Before the first day of school, first jobs, camp, and any family get together, Dad always said, "Just be yourself and everything will be fine." Same goes for generating rapport with prospects and customers. Before you consider the various ways we outline in the rest of this chapter to make connections with people, remember that it all starts with your genuine approach. Be genuine. Be yourself. Don't try to be anything you are not; don't create a new persona; and don't adopt a saleslike tone. Relax, smile, and go in with a positive attitude. Good things will follow. As Oscar Wilde said, "Be yourself; everyone else is already taken."

Be warm and friendly. Chilly people get chilly reactions from other people. Approach rapport building with the intent to be warm and friendly. Smile, give a firm handshake, make eye contact, and be engaged.

Show interest. No surprise to anyone, people are self-focused. This is quite helpful to those of us in complex sales situations because we need to learn about our prospects before we can provide the best solutions. Show interest in prospects as people as well as in their business challenges. Use their names when you speak with them and write to them.

Don't seem too needy. Most of us have seen someone who wanted to be liked, so he "tried hard," but it has the opposite effect. In trying to be liked, he appeared needy and conspicuous. There's something not "cool" when someone tries to force rapport. Show interest, but act subservient or be overly friendly and you will only turn the other person off. Don't come on like gangbusters.

Give genuine compliments. Sycophants get nowhere, but genuine compliments are endearing. If you like the office, someone's web site, or are impressed with their book, say so. If you saw in a press release that a prospect got a recent promotion, give him your congratulations. My grandmother always said, "Everyone needs to be stroked." She'd have made it as a social scientist.

Calibrate the rapport to "just right." New salespeople are overly sensitive to spending the time of a potential buyer. They often think, "I have an hour for this meeting and she's a CEO of a midsized company. I need to use the whole time to get my points across. No time for chitchat." From the administrative staff right on up to the CEO, buyers want to know that you're a real person before they will buy from you.

If you jump right in at the beginning of a meeting with the "Okay, let's get down to business" kickoff before you give everyone a chance to take a breath and say hello, it creates a tense atmosphere. You have to gauge when to start talking business—too early and a chilly abruptness fills the air. Too much time chatting and the buyer wonders, "Are we ever going to get moving?" Find the "just right" amount of nonbusiness conversation in your rainmaking conversation.

In our work with our clients at RAIN Group, we often assist in their sales conversations with their prospects. Not too long ago, we participated in a sales meeting for a technology product provider (our client) with the management team of a buttoned-down investment banking firm (our client's prospect). We were the third of three companies presenting that day and had arrived a little early for our meeting. Through the glass window into the conference room, we could see one of our competitors walking through their dog-and-pony show scheduled to end at noon. Noon came and went, then 12:15 . . . 12:20 . . . 12:27 . . . until finally they walked out.

After a five-minute break we were ushered in. Following normal introductions, our client asked the managing partner, who was looking a little tired and frustrated, "I know we have an hour, but if we can get through our presentation by 1:05 so you can get back on schedule would that help?" The managing partner replied, "If you can get done in 30 minutes, I will buy you all lunch!"

After 25 minutes, our client noted that he was five minutes from the end of the 30-minute time frame, then asked if his prospect had anything they needed to hear that we hadn't covered. The response: "Thank you for your sensitivity to our time. This is good stuff, let's keep going."

We ended up going through lunch. The meeting ended. We left. Our client had established both rapport *and trust* by promising and delivering on a timely presentation, and showing concern for the client. Ultimately, the prospect agreed to buy our client's products.

Read the culture. We recently spoke with Tony Hsieh, CEO of Zappos. At the time of this writing, Zappos has more than $1 billion in revenue and has been named regularly to *Forbes* magazine's list of the top 100 places to work. During our conversation, we asked Tony about the criteria Zappos use in their vendor selection and purchasing process. Here's what he had to say:

"Obviously they need to be capable of delivering the actual product itself. Once that criterion is met, we definitely look at how closely their values are aligned with our corporate core values. We really look for as close a culture or values match as possible. There are many cases where we actually choose to work with a provider who is not the lowest price, and may even be significantly more expensive than the next one down, just because it's going to be a better culture fit."[2]

Tony went on to say that during the company's hiring processes, managers check with receptionists, drivers, and other people on staff to see how friendly and warm the person was to them. Every touch point with a prospect organization is a chance to build rapport.

Let's say you take a read on a culture and see that there are some ways you might tailor your approach. We would not suggest that you change who you are to fit that culture. You can, however, send people to lead the meeting who might be a better fit than others. You could send a young team or a seasoned team, you could send one person or five, you

---

[2]RainToday.com "An Interview with Tony Hsieh" *Marketing and Selling Podcast* (2009) www.raintoday.com/pages/6155_podcast_episode_74_employee_happiness_ key_to_driving_profit_and_growth.cfm.

could send someone who's more "serious, down to business," or someone more cheery and enthusiastic.[3]

Without changing who you are, you can make conscious decisions that will make a difference. Do you wear a gray suit, white shirt, and red tie? Khakis and a button-down shirt with no tie? Or jeans and a T-shirt that says, "Talk nerdy to me." These kinds of decisions can make a big difference in making a connection, assuming you are still being true to yourself.

Balance advocacy and inquiry. One of the best ways to establish a connection with buyers is to balance asking questions (inquiry) with talking about your offerings or giving advice (advocacy). Talk too much and the prospect will tune out. Ask too many questions and they'll feel like they're getting the third degree. The rapport-building sweet spot is usually somewhere in the middle, leaning a bit toward giving the prospect more airtime than you.

One of the most powerful ways you can advocate that builds rapport is to tell stories. Great stories build your credibility and take people on an emotional journey. Good storytellers are endearing.

Listen actively. In our research report mentioned earlier, the single most prevalent problem that buyers reported encountering with sellers is sellers who don't listen. If your prospects perceive that you are not listening, building real rapport will be virtually impossible. Although the intro for this paragraph is "listen actively" it could just as easily be, "listen, actually." Many sellers are too caught up in what they're saying or too focused on what they are going to say next that they actually stop listening. Tune into what your prospect is saying and tune out everything else.

Show relevance, share similarities. People are attracted to people who are relevant and similar to them. Although we picked on the insincere fish-talk metaphor earlier in this chapter, the underlying concept is sound: The more alike two people are, the more they feel they have in common, the more apt they are to like each other. Demonstrating business relevance is equally as powerful as personal similarity. If you've worked in the same types of businesses, conquered the same types of challenges, and are well-versed in the same types of content, you'll find that everything you have in common will help form bonds of rapport and trust.

---

[3] For more on understanding and reading buyer work styles and preferences, visit www.RainGroup.com/booktools.

Turning Around a Challenging Situation

In our daily work in sales, we've all faced the situation where someone at our prospect's or customer's organization either won't give us the time of day, or we get the sense that they don't like us.

A common strategy to win them over is to reach out and give them something. This can work, but it can make people feel pandered to, and that just increases their standoffishness. Ben Franklin found himself in a similar situation in the Pennsylvania legislature. Here's how he approached it:

"I did not, however, aim at getting his favor by paying any servile respect to him, but, after some time, took this other method. Having heard that he had in his library a certain very scarce and curious book, I wrote a note to him, expressing my desire of perusing that book, and requesting he would do me the favor of lending it to me for a few days. He sent it immediately, and I return'd it in about a week with another note, expressing strongly my sense of the favor. When we next met in the House, he spoke to me (which he had never done before), and with great civility; and he ever after manifested a readiness to serve me on all occasions, so that we became great friends, and our friendship continued to his death. This is another instance of the truth of an old maxim I had learned, which says, "He that has once done you a kindness will be more ready to do you another, than he whom you yourself have obliged."[4]

Should you find yourself in a selling situation where you are having trouble breaking the ice or making the connection with someone, try reaching out and seeing if they'll do something for you. It will take some research to find out what that might be, but asking them to do you a kindness can be the key to the thaw.

[4]Franklin, B. 1900. *The Autobiography of Ben Franklin* (J. Bigelow, ed.). Philadelphia: Lippincott. (Originally published in 1868).

Questions that Build Rapport

There are so many questions you can ask that build rapport. As you ask them, keep in mind the first rapport-building tip in this chapter: Be genuine. If you ask questions sincerely, you'll get sincere answers and begin to build relationships. If you sound contrived, you won't.

- How was your weekend? Anything interesting?
- It was good to hear the short version of your background at the meeting, but since we're out for lunch, I'd love to get the long version. What's your story?
- I have to say, I really like your (insert something about them . . . their lobby, the artwork on their walls, how friendly their staff is, or anything else you actually liked, then ask an open-ended question about that particular thing).
- Are you from this area? Oh, interesting. I know people in . . . do you know (this person)? I've never been there, but I heard it's got . . . the most amazing restaurants . . . the most amazing scenery . . . the most amazing fly-fishing.
- Welcome to town. Have you been to Scottsdale before? Where are you staying? What's that like? A lot different from Vancouver, wouldn't you say?

Willy Loman said in *Death of a Salesman*, "The man who makes an appearance in the business world, the man who creates a personal interest, is the man who gets ahead. Be liked and you will never want." Sure, not everything worked out for Willy the way he might have wanted it to. He needed a lot more than being well-liked in order to succeed.

Many sellers, however, should take a page from Willy's book. Being liked won't win you the accounts, but it sure does help.

6

Aspirations and Afflictions

Research is formalized curiosity. It is poking and prying with a purpose.

—Zora Neale Hurston

Problems, frustration, pain, irritations, challenges . . . call them what you will, a salesperson must uncover his prospective client's afflictions. Once you've established rapport with a client, you have the opportunity to begin the process of learning what issues the prospect has and how you can help.

Uncovering afflictions is a crucial step in the selling process. The reasons are simple:

- If the prospect communicates his business afflictions to you, then it is likely that he will want them to go away if it's possible, and if it makes sense to invest the time, money, and mindshare to get rid of them.
- Each affliction you uncover gives you the chance to explore it fully to discover its true business impact.
- The more you openly discuss afflictions with prospects, the more those afflictions take front-and-center space in the prospect's mind.
- Uncovering and discussing one affliction can lead—much like brainstorming—to other afflictions of which the prospect may not have been thinking in the first place.

59

- If no business problems explicitly afflict the decision maker, inertia will keep her from doing anything that rocks the boat, including purchasing from you. If, however, you unearth a latent affliction or set of afflictions, you create desire in your prospective client to do something about them.

Once you've established rapport with the prospect and then uncovered afflictions, you have created an initial value gap: a perception that the buyer isn't where he wants to be or could be.

But afflictions are only half the story.

Uncovering afflictions is only half the story because afflictions only focus on half—the negative half—of customer needs. If you focus only on the negative, you leave opportunities on the table to expand your existing relationships and generate new opportunities.

The best way to understand why this is true is to think about how buyers buy. There are two core buyer mind-sets you will encounter when selling: *problem solving*, and *future seeking*.

Buyers are in problem-solving mode when something is bothering them or not performing up to expectations. When it gets to a point when they want to fix it, they seek out products or services to do so (or they accept marketing and sales overtures from providers to discuss their offerings). When you encounter this buying mind-set, your task is to uncover afflictions and help solve those afflictions with your products and services.

When buyers are future seeking, they're looking to grow, make their companies or personal lives better, or somehow improve their current circumstances, often looking for new and innovative ways to do so. In other words, maybe what's keeping them up at night is not a problem at all, but the passion and excitement that stem out of innovation, growth, success, and an endless list of possibilities.

Consider this example. You are a partner at a diversified accounting, financial, and business advisory firm. You have a meeting scheduled with the owner of a medium-sized business because he is not happy with the tax accounting services he is receiving from his current CPA firm. Through a series of questions, you have uncovered several problems this business owner has with his current accounting firm, including missed deadlines, impersonal service, and a suspicion that the firm isn't up-to-date on the latest tax regulations.

Because you know your firm specializes in his industry, and because of your dedication to exceptional client service, you know you stack up well. You ask him if he's facing particular problems and you get straight answers. Now you know how you can help. You continue the conversation, proposing next steps on how to move forward. You feel confident in how you managed the sales conversation and believe that a new client will be in your future.

You are just about to say good-bye when he says, "I'm meeting my company's lawyer for lunch. You two don't know each other. Want to join us?" Not wanting to pass up an opportunity to further the relationship (and because he eats at expensive French restaurants), you are happy to oblige.

You get to lunch, exchange pleasantries all around, and sit down to eat. A few minutes into the conversation the lawyer asks your potential client:

- "So, what's going on at your company lately?"
- "What do you want to get done in the next year or so?"
- "What are your stretch goals for the business?"
- "What do you think you need to do to get these things done?"
- "What don't you know yet that you need to find out?"
- "Parts of this conversation we had six months ago. What do you think you need to change to actually get it done this time?"

These questions are focused on future seeking (aspirations), not problem solving (afflictions). They open an entire new range of desires. You are amazed by some of your potential client's answers. You find he has opened up, going on for good chunks of time about the major initiatives at his company, including some initiatives he has not yet launched.

As you listen, you realize there are at least three areas within these strategic initiatives for which your expertise is a perfect fit and where your firm can help him greatly. One such initiative—valuing a niche company he's thinking about acquiring and managing the acquisition—is your personal expertise and passion! And the size of the fees in these areas is three times as large as what you just talked about in your meeting with the prospect only an hour before.

Capturing Missed Opportunities

What happened? How did you not uncover these opportunities earlier?

During the initial sales meeting, you focused on uncovering and solving the customer's afflictions. You did a good job of learning about the buyer's pain and found out how you could help.

During the lunch meeting, the lawyer focused not on the buyer's afflictions, but on his aspirations. And by doing so, he uncovered a whole other set of needs that you neglected to bring to the surface. He focused on the second half of your client's needs—the positive, the future, and the possibilities. The initial value gap is more than twice as large as it was when you only uncovered and articulated his afflictions. See Figure 6.1.

Uncovering Aspirations and Afflictions

Uncovering aspirations and afflictions is often short-changed and performed poorly. To help you uncover the largest value gap possible and succeed with discovering prospect needs, keep in mind the following guidelines.

Know the Range of Needs

Perhaps the most common factor missing in needs discovery is the lack of a systematic approach. Most customers in a specific industry, with a specific title, and of a specific size have a common set of possible needs waiting for you to uncover them.

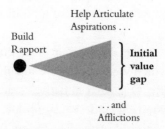

**Figure 6.1 Uncover aspirations and afflictions
to create an initial value gap.**

In Chapter 16, we outline how you can create a systematic approach to understanding client needs, from labeling of general needs categories, to listing specific needs in each category, to preparing questions that can uncover each need.

Preparing this type of client needs analysis before any discovery meeting is crucial to a successful sales conversation. Your preparation may be quick and simple because the range of your prospects' needs is small and easy to understand, or it may be complex because your prospect's needs are wide-ranging and elaborate. Whatever the case for you, it is imperative that you do not skip this stage of preparation.

When you're preparing for your meeting, your research will also uncover trigger events and background information that can get you started. Trigger events are those occurrences that signal a client may be in problem-solving or future-seeking mode. Trigger events can be a merger, a new competitor entering the field, expansion plans, reorganization, product launch, starting of a new strategy, new senior personnel, and so on.

Ask Questions that Uncover Needs and Wants

Yes, it's as simple as asking questions to uncover needs, but how you ask the questions is crucial. The first step is to use *broad, open-ended questions.* Questions like the following will get people to open up and start talking:

- "What is going on in your world these days?"
- "Can you give me a bit of background on what's happening regarding _____?" (insert category)
- "How have you approached these types of situations before?"
- "If you could wave your magic wand and make a few things happen, what would those things be?"

Broad open-ended questions are great for uncovering what the buyer currently perceives to be her set of needs. In other words, the buyer might share what she perceives to be her aspirations and afflictions without much prompting.

Here's an example of how this works from our own field of improving sales performance. You ask broad open-ended questions like those earlier and the prospect replies, "What's going on is that our salespeople don't have the skills to succeed. It's a big mix of skill gaps. Some can prospect and others can't. Some can close and others can't. Some maintain accounts for years while others need to constantly rebuild their pipelines because they don't have the repeat business they should. Others . . . I don't know, they seem to be doing the right things but the results just aren't there."

This prospect opened up the information floodgates immediately. It's not always this easy. Some buyers are guarded or simply don't share as much, so you will often need to move from these broad open-ended questions to *specific open-ended questions*.

When you ask specific open-ended questions, you will uncover latent needs—those needs the client may not even be aware of. Let's say you've uncovered that the buyer perceives her salespeople to have skill gaps, and she shares this with you. Skill gaps can hinder sales success greatly, but skills are just one area that affects sales performance.

Your questions then get more specific, but stay open-ended:

- "You've mentioned that you'd like to improve sales performance in general. There are a lot of ways to go about it along with skills and knowledge improvement. Let's start with your hiring process. How is that process working out for you?"
- "What about turnover? Can you outline the picture of how you are retaining your best salespeople?"
- "How well do you feel like your sales manager and sales management processes are working out? Where have they fallen short?"
- "How does your compensation structure drive the behaviors and outcomes that you're seeking to achieve?"

Any one of these questions will yield one of three answers:

1. Expression of need—"Now that I think of it, sales turnover has been killing us as well."
2. No perception of need—"I think sales turnover is just fine. It's better than industry average, at least."
3. Lack of knowledge—"I'm not sure, actually."

The third type of question to ask is the *specific closed-ended question*. Much of what is written about sales stresses asking open-ended questions and avoiding closed-ended questions. Closed-ended questions are great for diagnosis. It's easy, whether you get a yes or no answer, to follow up and get the prospect to elaborate.

Let's say you ask the question about the prospect's sales hiring processes noted above. She responds, "I think our hiring processes are working out pretty well, in fact."

You can then ask questions like:

- "Do you feel like you're hiring the best people fairly consistently?"
- "You're getting the pool of candidates you want when you're looking to hire, and you're getting them fast enough?"
- "You don't feel like you waste a lot of time sifting through the also-rans to get to the highest potential candidates?"
- "When you make offers, do the best candidates accept them as often as you would hope?"
- "Are you turning over more than 10 percent of your reps in the first three months?"
- "Do fewer than 80 percent of your new sales people succeed after one year?"

Although she might say things are "working out pretty well" at first, after you ask diagnostic closed-ended questions, she might start to see that it's not quite as good as she thought.

When you get an answer that you'd like to explore more fully, all you have to say is, "Can you tell me a little more about that?" or "How so?" and turn the closed-ended question into an open-ended one that continues to widen the value gap.

By asking closed-ended questions, you can uncover needs that prospects may not yet perceive as a problem, but when you ask the questions they reconsider. Also, by showing your prospects a better way in an area they may not perceive as a current need, you can generate the interest required to do something about it. For example:

You: "You sell a complex set of products and services. I can imagine it might take a while for new salespeople to get up to speed. How long does that take?"
Prospect: "About 12 to 18 months."

(continued)

You: "Yes, we see that as an average in this kind of industry."

Prospect: "That's what we hear as well, so I guess we're stuck with it."

You: "Not really. The average is 12 to 18 months because companies don't focus on improving it in the right way. But we've helped companies cut the ramp-up time in half, getting their salespeople up to speed and selling full tilt in 6 to 9 months . . . even sooner. Would you like to know more about how?"

Prospect: "I'll believe it when I see it, but sure."

The idea is to go from general to specific, uncovering prospects' own perceptions of their needs, helping them to express a broader set of needs, and finding out enough information so you can present ways they can improve that drive their interest and desire to act.

Advocating to Uncover Needs

Consultative sales-training methods typically focus heavily on diagnostic approaches to uncovering need. Ask questions, get answers, and that's that.

RAIN Selling shares some similarities with consultative sales-training methods, but we also believe strongly that the best rainmakers not only explore and build need through inquiry, they explore and build need through advocacy.

Rainmaker Principle 8 is to set the agenda, and be a change agent. Rainmakers start this process from the beginning during the diagnostic phase of selling.

This is not to say that rainmakers prescribe before they diagnose, but they bring research, ideas, knowledge of best practices, case studies, and other expertise that can help prospects see new paths to reaching their goals.

To continue with our earlier example, let's say the prospect would like to see how to cut down the time to full salesperson productivity by 50 percent. Your answer to that can be, "Let's do that, then. We have about 40 minutes left in this meeting. I think it would be a good idea to take, say, the next 20 or so and I can share that with you. Let me take a minute and open a presentation that will help me give you a sense of how to go about it."

Depending on how the meeting's going, this direction may distract from your core selling goal. If it does, you can suggest scheduling a follow-up meeting to take her through the presentation. Either way, if you can show her how she can cut down the time to full productivity, you know you can then show a huge impact on the top and bottom line. Assuming your process is compelling, you can find yourself with a willing buyer because you set the agenda and helped her see the business merits of doing something she otherwise wasn't even considering.

Not Going How You Want? Reverse Direction

Let's say you find a prospect who is unwilling to disclose any needs. They say, "No, don't have that problem. No, can't say we've seen much of a challenge there. Yes, we're happy with the people we've worked with. Saw your presentation, but don't think there's anything in there that applies to us." And so on.

Now is a good time to see if you should disengage while, at the same time, giving you a good chance to actually uncover need. To do this, try reversing direction.

Reversing direction changes the flow and tone of where the conversation is heading. In this situation, reversing direction means discontinuing your needs discovery, and checking with the prospect if that's where he wants to go.

It is a salesperson's job to be comfortable making their customers uncomfortable. If you can't get your customer uncomfortable at times and be okay with that, you're never going to make it. You have to be willing to ask the tough questions. When I'm having a conversation with someone about something, I ask, "Hey, do me a favor. Talk to me. How's this process going to go? Who else is involved? What influence do they have? Are there other people who could derail this?" I mean, there's a million different questions depending upon the situation and the customer.

—Jim Keenan, Vice President, North American Sales, Pace

You can say to him, "It seems like you have a lot going for you. That's good to hear. Perhaps you're just in a better situation than most of the people that we speak to. I've asked a number of questions aimed at seeing what's up regarding sales performance, and what I've heard is that everything is just where you want it to be. If that's the case, perhaps we should disengage the conversation. I wouldn't want to take more of your time or mine if there's nothing down the path. If you're sure everything is up to where you want it to be, we should stop now."

At this point, the prospect is probably surprised. You're a salesperson and he's a busy executive. You've been doing your thing and he's been resisting (or he really perceives no aspiration or affliction in the area you're discussing). He expected you to keep pressing until he ended the call, but *you* don't want to waste *your* time.

Maybe your prospect wasn't done yet. Maybe there was something on his mind but for whatever reason you just didn't uncover it yet.

One of two things will happen now:

1. Perceiving no possibility of aspiration of affliction: "You're right, I think stopping now is a good idea, but we should stay in touch in case something comes up."
2. Perceiving that he might miss an opportunity: "No, no, I think we should continue talking. There may be something; I'm just not sure we're there yet. I'm trying to put my finger on it."

Either way you win. If it's time to be done, it's time. You can look back later and analyze if there was something more you should have done to generate interest and desire, and uncover aspirations and afflictions. Maybe so and maybe not, but this one is over and you can move on. If the buyer expresses a desire to continue, it's likely there's some incongruity in his mind between where he is and where he wants to be. There's a value gap there, you just haven't defined it. Now you have license for more time to figure out what that is. And, as a bonus, you probably gained some respect from the prospect with your up-front approach.

The trick to uncovering aspirations and afflictions is to not over-complicate it, but not miss anything either.

- Know the range of potential customer aspirations and afflictions based on the customer needs profile.
- Inquire—Ask three different types of diagnostic questions—broad open-ended questions, specific open-ended questions, and closed-ended questions—that uncover needs and wants.
- Advocate—share ideas and stimulate thinking—to uncover additional needs.
- Make latent needs explicit.
- Maintain patience to explore all opportunities.
- Avoid closing off the conversation too quickly by jumping to conclusions.

Uncovering aspirations and afflictions is no more than formalized research. Poke and prod with a purpose, and expand your rainmaking success.

7 | Impact

What have you done for me lately?

—Janet Jackson

After you uncover the prospect's aspirations and afflictions, you are ready to take your rainmaking conversation to the next level—a level that many salespeople fail to achieve. By moving to this next level you immediately separate yourself from those who don't.

The idea is to figure out the answer to "So what?" regarding all of the aspirations and afflictions you've uncovered. If the prospect's afflictions don't get resolved, so what? What won't happen that they *want* to happen? Will things get worse? How will these afflictions affect the bottom line of the prospect's company, division, or department? How will letting the unresolved afflictions fester affect the prospect's life?

If prospects' aspirations don't become reality, so what? Will they fall by the wayside never to be picked up again? If they do become reality, how much better will prospects' competitive positions become? How much more will they personally succeed?

The exact "so what" questions will vary depending on the situation, but your ability to quantify and paint the "so what" picture is the cornerstone for making it clear to the prospect just how important buying from you is. Creating urgency for buying hinges on how well you help your client see the "so what" picture.

Answering "So what?" will uncover the impact you can have on a customer's life and business. When you calculate the impact of helping

71

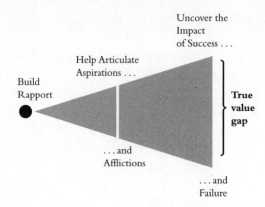

Figure 7.1   True Value Gap

prospects realize their aspirations and solve their afflictions, you establish a
new baseline for where prospects *could* be. When you understand the impact
caused by prospects' afflictions, you establish the true business obstacles that
they present. Take this all into account—the cost of failure and the benefits
of success—and you have now established the true value gap. See Figure 7.1.

Two Types of Impact

Impact comes in two flavors, *rational* and *emotional*, and they work closely
together.

The rational impact is the business case—where a prospect understands
the return on investment (ROI) of solving particular afflictions or achieving
aspirations.

The emotional impact is the prospect's desire for success, financial freedom, peer recognition, pride, happiness, stress reduction, and so on. These are
powerful forces in buying, and they're often underestimated by salespeople.

Show someone a way to succeed more, solve problems, and make more
money, and all of a sudden that person feels stress going away, the excitement
of making a difference, and the anticipation of greater success and worry-
free weekends that he hasn't had in years.

Demonstrate the rational impact, and you'll build the emotional impact.
Fail to show the business case, and you won't capture the prospect's interest
and desire, you won't take him on an emotional journey, and he won't feel
that it's important enough to put your agenda on the top of his to-do list.

Make the Impact Tangible

Until you clarify the impact, prospects won't likely know what the value of working with you will ultimately be.

The idea is to make the impact as tangible and measurable as possible. To do that, you need to:

- Calculate and communicate the rational impact.
- Clarify and communicate the emotional impact.
- Assess and communicate the impact of change against the status quo.
- Maximize a sense of urgency for moving forward.
- Build credibility with examples of similar impact.

Calculate and communicate the rational impact in dollars. Each affliction that you solve and each aspiration that you help customers realize will have some kind of financial impact. Whenever possible, you should make the case for the financial effects of buying from you.

To calculate the dollar impact, you need to know your cost, the relative costs and benefits of the alternatives, and your impact model. Understanding the cost of your products and services is something most people have a good handle on. Understanding the cost of the alternatives and your impact model both warrant further exploration.

Companies that exceed buyers' expectations in their ability to sell value achieve 6 percent more of their overall revenue plans than companies that fall short of buyers' expectations. Simply put, if you can sell value, you will command higher prices.[1]

Let's start with the latter. Your *impact model* is made up of the set of assumptions about how buying from you will be of financial benefit to the customer. Understanding your impact model is especially helpful when you try to convince buyers of the benefits of taking a particular action that they might not currently be considering.

Here's an example of how this works.

---

[1] CSO Insights, "Sales Performance Optimization Report: Sell Cycle Review Analysis," 16.

The offering is Insurance Archaeology and Settlement of Insurance Claims. What, you say? You have no idea what insurance archaeology is? Neither do almost all of the potential buyers—that is, until the company that offers these services, let's call them Insurance Archaeology, Inc. (IAI), contacts them. Then the prospects buy it regularly.

IAI works with businesses more than 50 years old in a select group of industries to find money due to them by insurance companies that the companies never knew about. For example, let's say that in 1999 the company settled an environmental lawsuit against them that cost them $15 million.

What they didn't know was that in 1971 the CFO at the time purchased insurance to cover the company against this kind of claim.

With insurance archaeology, IAI can, over the course of a year or so, uncover all the insurance policies that the company in question has ever taken out. For this, IAI requires a $12,000 per month retainer for the year, or $144,000.

On average, IAI reclaims between $10 million and $40 million for its clients. Along with the $12,000 per month retainer, the firm takes 15 percent of the payments the insurance firms receive. For IAI, the impact model is simple:

Cost: $144,000 plus 15 percent of money reclaimed.

Benefit: "Found" money from legitimate, but forgotten, claims on their insurance policies.

Low estimate: $10 million reclaimed	High estimate: $40 million reclaimed
Cost: $144,000 plus $1.5 million (15 percent of reclaimed money) = $1.65 million	Cost: $144,000 plus $6 million = $6.15 million
Return for client: $8.35 million ROI = 506 percent	*Return for client: $33.85 million* ROI = 550 percent

The total risk for the client is less than $150,000. The likely return is somewhere between $8 million and $35 million. The impact model is compelling for any company that meets the base criteria for insurance archaeology.

Companies rarely consider engaging this kind of undertaking until IAI reaches out to them. Assuming that the IAI salesperson can capture attention and create enough interest to find out what possibilities exist, it's difficult to see how a prospect company wouldn't put insurance archaeology on the radar screen as a priority. The impact is unbelievably compelling.

Not all impact models are this straightforward, but most products and services have specific financial benefits that can be gained from their purchase. You need to understand the various factors of how your offering can impact a business if you want to be able to build an ROI case for a prospect and communicate it to them.

Common business factors that affect financial impact are:

- Reduced cycle times
- Increased uptime
- Lower risk
- Faster time to market
- Increased salesperson performance
- Strengthened innovation
- Higher profitability
- Less waste
- Increased leads in the pipeline
- Lower cost in any area while maintaining or improving quality
- Better quality/fewer repairs/longer life
- Increased brand recognition or preference
- Less employee turnover
- Fewer stops and starts of projects
- Less scrap and rework
- More employee productivity

Each one of these areas, and many more not listed here, can be quantified. Your job is to quantify them and then make sure the prospect is keenly aware of the financial impact of working with you.

Clarify and communicate the emotional impact. Increased prestige. A more enjoyable day. Safety and security. Not working regularly until 9 PM anymore. The ability to finally take a vacation with peace of mind. Reduced stress. There are innumerable nonfinancial influences of buying from you that can tip the scales in your favor. Although you must communicate the impact in dollars clearly, you should also know what nonfinancial factors are in your favor and be able to communicate them.

Assess and communicate the impact against the alternative. The first step is to be certain that you know the primary alternatives (and realize it's not always a direct competitor) that the prospect is considering so you can make the most compelling case.

Consider, for example, a technology company selling the benefits of outsourcing technology support for small businesses may have, as a primary competitor, their prospects' decisions to hire their own staff.

Let's say an IT leader at a firm with 25 lawyers has a salary of $75,000, and that leader just left the firm. The firm is considering hiring a new leader for this position at the same salary. The technology outsourcing company charges $60 per month per desktop to support each user by remote access (the firm has 50 users). That's $720 per user per year plus about $10,000 per server (and the firm has two servers), and $20,000 for additional services such as on-site maintenance, software installs, and technology strategy meetings with CIO level technologists.

The technology outsourcing firm's impact model looks like this:

Hire internally	Outsource
$75,000 per year for IT leader/desktop support manager	$20,000 per server
	$20,000 on-site tech fees
	$36,000 in user support fees
	Total cost = $76,000

Looking at it like this, the firm leaders might say, "Well, it would be better if we had someone on-site to help us do whatever we need. If we want to install a new server we don't have to pay another $10,000 in fees plus the cost of installing it. And if we have someone working here, they will feel more connected to the organization and we'll have better service. Let's hire someone."

As it stands, there isn't much of a financial case to suggest switching to outsourcing. But if the salesperson knows his impact model, he will be able to uncover the impact for a particular client, communicate it clearly, and know how to compare much more favorably beyond what's on the surface.

The additional factors in the technology outsourcing firm's impact model are:

- Low incremental fee for each additional computer supported.
- No recruiting, staffing, HR, and overhead fees.
- Saved downtime at customer site.
- All levels of IT support expertise included.
- Expertise across a variety of technologies.
- Catastrophic failure coverage at no extra cost.
- Consistently superior service quality.

By exploring the impact model beyond the salary costs, with the potential client, the good salesperson can make a very different case for outsourcing.

Tips for Uncovering and Communicating Impact

To maximize urgency, ask, "What won't happen?" Good salespeople demonstrate strong impact for why their prospects should buy from them. Sometimes the impact seems so clear that the salesperson thinks, "This sale is in the bag . . . the value is so clear that it would be crazy if they didn't buy."

Yet even though the impact is clear to the salesperson, after the final sales meeting the prospect says he will follow up with him on Tuesday with a decision. Tuesday comes and goes. Wednesday and Thursday come and go. Still no decision.

Finally, on Friday, the customer tells the salesperson how impressed their team was with the presentation, but they've decided to delay any action for at least a quarter. Oh, and please keep in touch. There's no competitor on the account, no major assumptions or situations have changed, and they're not going to solve their problem themselves. They're just going to sit on it a while.

Impact Model Factor	Questions to Ask	Answer and Response	Impact
Low incremental fee for each additional computer supported	Q. What's your growth plan in terms of staff this year? Q. Did you know that industry standard user-to-tech support ratios are about one tech for 50 to 60 people?	A. We should be up to 65 or 70 people in the next 12 months A. No, I didn't.[2] Response: You'll probably need to hire another person at $45,000 or so to handle the extra load if you hire internally. With us, for 15 more users you'll add $10,800 in support fees.	Extra cost if we hire internally = $342,000
No recruiting, staffing, HR, and overhead fees	Q. What are the additional costs of hiring tech person?	A. 20 percent benefits and overhead = $15,000 10 percent bonus = $7,500 25 percent recruiter fee = $16,750 Hassle of interviewing many people	Extra cost if hire internally = $41,250
Saved downtime at customer site	Q. How quickly was the average response time to user issues? How quickly were emergencies handled?	A. Average response time to general issues was 4 hours or so. If something was critical, it was usually handled quickly, but if two emergencies came up, and they did here and there, one person would have to wait. Every once in a while, there would be a backup because our IT person was dealing with something sticky, and there would be a line of people waiting for help. On average, all of our 25 lawyers and our support staff as well have some kind of issue every month.	25 lawyers × 2 hours lost per month × $250 an hour = $12,500 per month in lost billable time due to technical issues. $150,000 in billable hours

[2] www.zdnet.com/videos/whiteboard/users-to-tech-support-ratio/155252

Saved downtime at customer site	Q. Let's say, then that each person loses 3 of those 4 hours they're waiting for tech support on average. Is that fair? And your average billable rate for your lawyers is $250 an hour? A. Yes and yes. Response: With us, there's no wait. Call in and get a tech to help you within 15 seconds on average. Emergencies are handled right away, all the time, with multiple capabilities to handle multiple emergencies at once if needed. We can get issues resolved faster while cutting down wait time and can save your staff at least two of the three hours they're losing with your current in-house strategy.	saved per year working with us.
Expertise across a variety of technologies	Q. Did you ever need to use outside IT support because your internal person didn't have a particular expertise? If so, what was it and how much did it cost? A. Yes, Jim was great with the networking and the desktop support, but when we need to work on our security and firewall, we bring in a tech security person. That usually costs about $10,000 per year. Response: We have experts in that technology, and 22 other major business technologies that might crop up. We can do this work from remote without extra fees.	$10,000 saved
Catastrophic failure coverage at no extra cost	Q. Have you ever had a server failure and needed to scramble to get the whole A. Yes, it happened two years ago when we got hacked. We had to call in extra help to get back online. Meanwhile, the whole	10 billable hours per person × 25 people × $250

(continued)

Impact Model Factor	Questions to Ask	Answer and Response	Impact
	company back online through a tough issue?	company had tech issues and got no support. It took us a week before we had it all sorted out. Must have cost us 10 billable hours per person and $10,000 in emergency tech help.	per hour = **$62,500 billable hours lost.**
		Response: With us, if you get hacked or your systems go down without warning, we will call in the cavalry, making sure a team of people is working 24/7 to get the company back online, and support all the users with our desktop techs to get everyone individually working. We'd cut that downtime in half and save the additional $10,000 in extra tech labor.	We'd cut that in half, **saving $31,250** in lost billable hours, and **saving $10,000** in extra tech labor.
Service quality	Q. How happy was your team with the service they had with past IT support staff?	A. Mixed. He did what he wanted. Sometimes people got the service they needed, and other times people waited until he was ready.	And I got all the complaints.

Total saved with us	$34,000 in labor saved as you grow.
	$41,000 saved in HR costs.
	$150,000 saved in billable hours waiting for support.
	$10,000 saved in tech security labor.
	$41,000 ($31,000 lost billable hours, and $10,000 in extra labor) likely saved in server meltdown.
	$276,000 benefit in working with us.
	Plus, we won't quit, we offer more flexibility as you grow, we have broader and deeper knowledge of different technologies than anyone you could hire, and we have a 98.8 percent satisfaction rating with our clients.

To understand these situations, you must first take a look at the customer's true options in buying your products and services. The customer can usually take three paths:

1. Get help to fix the problem by buying something.
2. Fix the problem on her own.
3. Do nothing at all.

Often the salesperson will demonstrate strong impact. And the customer may well agree that the value proposition is solid. However, for some reason, the customer has no sense of urgency and chooses to do nothing at all.

At this point, you don't know what can turn the situation around. You do know for certain that the client has chosen to table the issue, and that the current window of opportunity on this sale has closed.

The next time you are selling, if you sense any lack of urgency on the part of the prospect to buy, ask, "What won't happen?"

- *Ask yourself, "What won't happen?"* Near the end of the sales process you should have a solid idea of how your offerings will provide value to your potential customer if they buy them. Your next step is to get them to understand what the impact of *not* choosing to engage you will be.

  Build a case to yourself for the negative impact for the customer if they choose not to solve their problems or address their issues. Armed with this analysis, you are ready for the next action.

- *Ask the prospect, "What won't happen?"* At the appropriate time in the sales process, usually as you sense they do not see the issue as a top priority, ask the prospect, "Can you give me a sense of what you think would happen if you choose *not* to move forward in this process and engage us?" Like a good trial lawyer, you already know from your earlier analysis what those impacts will be.

  If the prospect doesn't enumerate what won't happen as specifically as you might like, lead them with further questions. For example, the middle part of the conversation might go like this:

Salesperson: "Yes, I can see what you're saying about monthly revenue generation taking a potential $70,000 hit if you don't take care of this, that's $840,000 per year. I am also wondering what will happen to your customer retention. Since you're retaining 50 percent of your customers per year and we've already discussed how engaging us can get you up to about 60 percent retention, what might happen if we don't go forward?"

Prospect: "We'll, I'm not really sure. We've been losing a little ground to competitors, which is, of course, why we're talking here. So I guess we'd lose a little more. But I don't know how much."

Salesperson: "It's impossible to know for certain, of course, but do you think it's more than 2 percent . . . 5 percent . . . higher?"

Prospect: "I'd guess, no, I'm pretty sure, it would be more than 5 percent, but not sure how much."

Salesperson: "Okay, then, we'll use 5 percent as a benchmark, to be on the conservative side. One last question about pricing; what do you see happening there?"

Prospect: "Well, if we move forward, we'd like to raise prices, of course, but if we don't move forward, we'll continue to have price competition pressures. I think we'll find our prices either hold steady or fall by up to 3 percent."

- *Quantify the results:* Just as you quantify the benefits and value of moving forward as a part of the RAIN Selling process, quantify the impact for the customer of not moving forward. In this scenario, calculate the financial value of each percent of customers that the prospect retains from one year to the next. Calculate the effect of losing the price competition battle. Calculate the effect of losing ground to competitors. Make sure your case is clear before going on to the next step.

- *Demonstrate the results:* When you demonstrate your value in conversation, presentation, or proposal, also demonstrate the results of the "What Won't Happen?" analysis.

Take care to translate percentages and other metrics to dollar amounts. Also keep in mind the best metrics to use are the ones your prospect is already using or agrees on.

By employing a "What Won't Happen?" analysis in your sales process, you will find a consistent increase in the sense of urgency with your clients, resulting in measurably increased close rates.

Build credibility and reduce risk with similar impact. They have aspirations and afflictions. You have capabilities to help them meet their goals. The value proposition is clear, but they are still unsure. Sometimes they want to know if you've been there before. And, when you were there, what happened. The right story or case study can be a powerful demonstrator of impact and a strong positive influence on the sale.

For example, you might say, "You have three things going on here. First, you haven't been able to translate your product marketing materials and technical guides into the 12 different languages of the various countries you're selling into in less than five months. Second, you've discovered a number of translation issues have created confusion in overseas markets, pegging you as an outsider. Third, you're working with six separate vendors to get all of your translations completed."

"These three points are almost the exact same situation that we ran into at XYZ company that also sells a technical product into eight overseas markets. After we started working with them, we got translation time down from five to two months, implemented a translation quality assurance program that reduced monthly reported errors from 450 to about 60, and, of course, they only have to deal with one vendor: us."

"They told us last month that the three months saved plus the stronger connection to the local markets with better language translation has increased sales in each market by about 7 percent. For them, that's about $8 million annually."

Demonstrate impact tangibly: The more you can make the impact tangible, the stronger the case for the impact will be. In essence, you need to paint a picture for them so they can see, as tangibly as you can depict it, what is going to change for them if they engage your services or buy your product.

To do this, you must paint a picture of the New Reality.

8 | New Reality

I can't describe it, but . . .

. . . I know it when I see it.

—Potter Stewart, Associate Justice, United States Supreme Court

In his ruling in *Jacobellis v. Ohio*, Justice Stewart probably sounded like many of the clients with whom you work. Until they experience it, clients often have a difficult time knowing exactly what they are buying and what value they will receive.

One of the most important skills in selling is helping potential clients understand the outcomes they get when they buy. Whatever your offering may be, it will somehow change your clients' world. In other words, you will create a *new reality* for them.

Establish the New Reality Benchmark

At the end of a well-managed sales process, your job is to create a new reality that is best for your customers, taking into account their specific aspirations and afflictions and the impact of doing something about them.

The new reality process should start before you craft the solution. Ask potential customers what they want the world to look like after they work with you. A good way to get the creative juices flowing is to ask broad questions that encourage envisioning the future.

According to CSO, a salesperson's ability to align his solution with the buyer's needs will significantly increase his ability to get closer to commitment from the buyer.[1]

- In six months, when the products are fully installed, what would need to happen for you to consider it a success?
- What isn't your current provider delivering that you need?
- What do you want to have happen as a result of our work together?
- How do you see the implementation of this technology solution improving your data maintenance?

Don't be surprised if the prospect's first answer to these questions is, "I don't know." Sometimes the prospect will say, "That's a good question," and then pause. If this happens, do not jump right in. Silence will indicate you will wait an answer. With some thought the prospect will start talking.

If you need to prompt him, you can say things like:

- Tell me what's coming to mind.
- Forget the big picture for a minute. You mentioned you hoped that X, Y, and Z would be better. Let's say they were better . . . much better . . . how would you describe this to a colleague if they asked you how it's going?
- Can you think of a competitor or another company that's more like what *you* want to be like in this area? Tell me about them.

One question you need to answer for yourself is *when* to establish a new reality benchmark. Sometimes, if you ask about the prospect's desired new reality and he doesn't have a context for what's possible, he gets frustrated because he doesn't know, or he establishes something completely unrealistic. If you find this happening to you, you should not dig in too deeply here until you *give* the buyer a sense of what you can do. For example, instead of probing up front to establish a new reality benchmark, lead the RAIN discussion in order, leaving new reality last. Along the way, you can share results you've helped others achieve.

---

[1]CSO Insights, "Sales Performance Optimization Report: Sales Execution Analysis," 11.

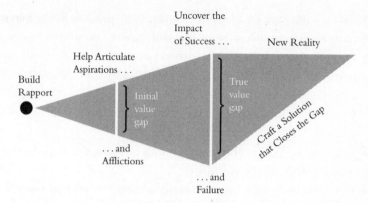

Figure 8.1   Create the New Reality Benchmark

That way, when you ask the buyer what he would like to see, you have already established a benchmark that you are confident you can deliver. The buyer's responses now are more likely to be realistic.

Craft Your Solution

Armed with your client's answers and the steps you have already taken during the RAIN process you can now craft a solution.

With this much customer knowledge, most salespeople believe that they can make a huge positive. They then write out (or simply tell the potential customer) a list of their offerings that will make the prospect's world a better place. However, the prospects don't yet see how you can help because you haven't connected the dots for them. All the good work the provider did in the sales conversations has yet to come into focus.

You, as the seller, must translate the new reality into dollars and cents, help buyers understand how their lives will be better if they purchase, and then, as compellingly as you can, paint the picture in which they see the difference between their undesirable current state and much improved new reality.

Communicate the New Reality

Whatever the new reality is, you need to describe it to the customer. For example, you might tell the customer that he will:

- Save 22 percent, or $120,000 on the cost of XYZ Widgets.
- Save $170 a month in bank fees and broker commissions.
- Improve the cycle times by 13 days by cutting out major inefficiencies in the operational process, which translates to $225,000 per month of costs saved.
- Improve quality levels by 17 percent and reduce defects by 22 percent.
- Improve revenue by $600,000 a month by increasing the effectiveness of lead generation programs.
- Eliminate the headaches of working with the current provider who is always late and difficult to reach.

Bullet points and prose, however, can only take you so far. Pictures, graphs, and charts can be quite powerful. The goal is to make the benefits of working with you crystal clear to the prospect.

It may be as simple as describing the current state, a few key factors that you'll change, and what the difference will look like in the future state. Let's say you're working to improve sales performance. The metrics in sales are fairly straightforward because you can measure sales results by person.

Thus, the new reality might look like Figure 8.2.

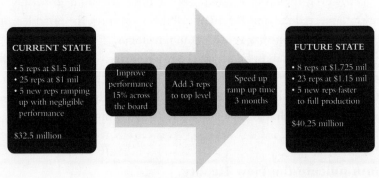

Increase: $7.75 million per year

Figure 8.2

Note that this graphic doesn't serve to describe *how* you will create these results. Perhaps you've already presented how you'll effect the changes necessary to produce the outcome. This picture does, however, paint the picture of the *outcome* you aim to produce.

Charts that outline the value your offerings will deliver to the client also work quite well. For example, you can take information from previously on page 78, and put it into the following format:

Category	Before	After
Adding 15 to 20 employees	Need to hire an additional $45,000 salaried technical support person plus benefits and recruiter cost	No need to hire a support person. Add 15 users for $10,800 with no additional HR costs. **Savings: $32,000 plus $10,000 benefits and $11,000 recruiter costs: Total savings of $53,000**
Etc.		
Etc.		

The simple before-and-after table is effective in helping people see the difference between where they are and where they want to be.

You do not have to rely on just one picture. You can, as appropriate, present the new reality in both qualitative (descriptive or conceptual) terms as well as quantitative (financial or other numerical-based measure).

Let's say that your goal is to redesign a messy process. You've already established in your needs discovery that the process is convoluted, longer than it needs to be, and full of waste. You can say to the client:

Your process is very similar to what we ran into at XYZ Company. Theirs looked like this (see Figure 8.3):

After about four weeks, when the redesign was completed, a new process producing the same result looked like this (see Figure 8.4):

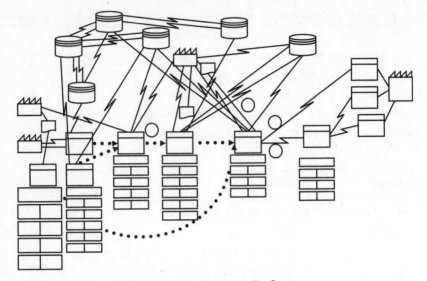

Figure 8.3   Process Before

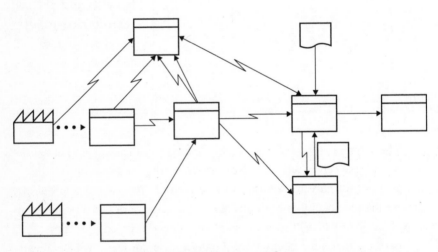

Figure 8.4   Process After

The new process was 40 percent faster than the old one, taking only 10 days when it used to take 18. We also helped this client use fewer outside resources because of the improved efficiencies, and this reduced the cost of the process by 50 percent. The original cost was about $2,000 each time the client had to go through the process, about 1,500 times per year. Now it costs $1,000 each time.

In other words:

Category	Before	After
Cycle time	18 days	10 days
		40 percent improvement
Cost savings	$2,000 per instance	$1,000 per instance
	1,500 instances	1,500 instances
	$3 million per year	**$1.5 million per year cost**
		$1.5 million per year savings Life of
		improvements plus or minus 4 years
		4 year savings: $6 million

At the same time, we reduced product defects by 34 percent. The new process produced better outcomes than the previous.

We were able to produce $6 million in savings over a four-year period for this client, and we believe we can do the same for you . . . with one difference. Since your process is more expensive for you to run, if we produce a similar percentage of savings, the four-year tally should be closer to $10 million.

The more you can create tables, graphs, and charts to help prospects understand the value and communicate it to colleagues, the more deals you will win.

Differentiate Your Offering, Substantiate Your Claims

As you present the new reality, buyers will be asking themselves three questions, questions that mirror the three legs of the value proposition stool:

1. Is it worth it to do this? (Resonate)
2. Are they the best option to help us get it done? (Differentiate)
3. Do I believe they can produce what they say they can produce? (Substantiate)

The answer to the first question will result in a go/no-go decision. To get a go decision, you must make sure you communicate the impact as clearly and compellingly as possible.

Let's assume that they've made the decision to go. If you're the only provider they're considering, the deal is yours unless you blow it. If, however, you have to compete with other providers, the balance of what you need to communicate will shift from impact of doing it at all to differentiating yourself from the other options the prospect has to help them address the issue.

As you present your new reality, you must communicate to the prospect why you're the best available option. At the same time, you need to get the prospect to believe that you'll do what you say you're going to do, and that working with you will be a good experience.

When you attend to the various components that people need to get a sense of what it's going to be like to work with you, and when you present your solutions graphically you help your situation in several ways:

- You'll reinforce that you understand their business.
- You'll reinforce that you understand their needs and that you listened.
- You'll be setting the agenda as a full partner in their success.
- The quality of your proposal will give them a sense of the quality of your products, your services, and your company.
- You'll differentiate yourself from the competition through the thoughtfulness and thoroughness of your process (many salespeople lose based on lack of effort—they just don't work hard enough in the sales process to prove their worth).
- When you deliver a WOW new reality picture, you endear yourself to clients that much more. They'll want to work with you versus other options.
- When you deliver a WOW new reality picture, you'll give the prospect the sense that you can deliver on your lofty promises. If you do it so well in the sales process, you can do it in product delivery.

Depending on the situation, there are a number of different new reality factors that may be important for you to communicate. See Figure 8.5.

The core factors are represented in the RAIN Group Sales Solution Model. Here are the various factors:

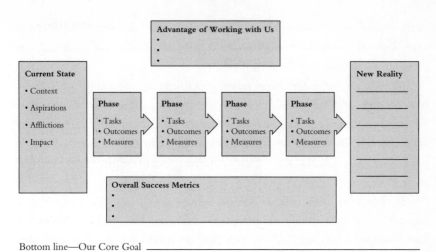

Figure 8.5   RAIN Group Sales Solution Model

- *Current state* where you describe what life is like for the prospect right now.
- *New reality* or future state, where you compare and contrast the difference between where prospects are now, and where they want to be.
- *Phases* or stages of what you'll do to help them get there, including who does what, what the outcomes of each phase should be, and the measures of how you know if you succeeded in each phase.
- *Advantages* where you describe why they'd want to choose you to produce these results versus the competition or doing it themselves internally.
- *Overall success metrics* where you summarize what it looks like when you've succeeded.
- *Bottom line* where you state the top priority in simple terms so everyone stays on the same page.

Depending on your situation, you will need to communicate some solution factors more strongly than others. For example, you may not have a phased approach to implementing your product or service. It may be simpler than that. You may have specific competitors vying for the contract, and your advantages section must then be robust and rock solid. Whatever the case, you can use the model to help you cover all your bases as you communicate your new reality.

Buying can be as difficult as selling. It's tough to get a handle on what to buy because it's difficult to visualize the impact, difficult to differentiate between competing products, services, and providers, and difficult to know who can actually deliver on what they say they will deliver. It's challenging for buyers to understand these factors themselves and communicate them to their colleagues.

If, however, you follow RAIN Selling and paint the picture of a compelling new reality, your prospects will want the solution, know the best provider is you, and believe that you can get the job done . . . because they will know it when they see it.

9

Balancing Advocacy and Inquiry

Ideal conversation should be a matter of equal give and take, but too often it is all "take."

—Emily Post

When sellers talk too much, they win too few customers. So why do so many sellers find themselves prattling away when they should be asking questions and listening? Emily could have been a sales consultant, as she pegs the sales chatterer just right in *Etiquette.*[1]

> The voluble talker—or chatterer—rides his own hobby straight through the hours without giving anyone else, who might also like to say something, a chance to do other than exhaustedly await the turn that never comes.

Although some salespeople talk too much, some talk too little. The voluminous teachings of people who subscribe to the school of consultative selling tell us that good salespeople ask great questions, spending much more time listening than talking.

Unfortunately, too many sellers take the advice too strongly and ask question after question, offering no advice and setting no agenda. They can

---

[1] Emily Post. *Etiquette.* 1922.

take it so far they make the person on the other side feel like they're getting the third degree. Instead of talking too much, they're asking too many questions. Busy executives don't have the time for answering question after question in hopes that, after spending a couple of hours with someone, the seller will come back with something worthwhile. This is especially true if you're selling a demand-driving service, and need to inspire them to put you on their agenda.

The key to talking the right amount is balancing advocacy (giving advice . . . setting the agenda . . . talking) and inquiry (asking questions . . . finding out more . . . letting the client have the air time).

Indeed, the "A" and the "I" in RAIN Selling serve a dual purpose. As we've learned, these letters stand for aspirations and afflictions, and impact, but they also double as a reminder to balance advocacy with inquiry.

Why We Talk Too Much

Many sellers go on and on when talking to prospects. They fall into the too-much-talk trap for one or more of the following reasons:

- *I need to show my expertise:* Of course you do. How else will prospects know if you are good at what you do? However, prospects want to know whether you are a good fit for working with them as much as they are evaluating whether they should trust your advice. If they sense you are too self-focused, they'll be turned off before you get far.
- *I need to persuade, pitch, and inspire:* This is likely true, and you should do it. But if you overdo it or time it wrong you'll alienate buyers.
- *I get nervous, so I talk:* If this is the case, explore why you are nervous. Are you not comfortable with sales conversations? Are you uncomfortable talking to senior level managers? Do you not know your offerings and the value they provide well enough? (By the way, many rainmakers felt like this when they first started selling. It's something you just have to overcome.)
- *I have no plan or objective:* As Mack Hanan would say, "If you don't have a plan, stay in the car." When you enter into sales conversations and you are not sure where you want to go or what you want to

accomplish, the conversation meanders all over the place and ends with neither clarity of purpose nor helpful action steps.

- *I easily get distracted:* Related to the previous point, if you don't have a plan or if you can't get back to the agenda at hand, you'll spend too much time off topic. Thus, any new topic that gets introduced in the sales conversation can lead you down time consuming and fruitless paths.

- *Enthusiasm is my style:* Yes, indeed, you may have a dynamic, effervescent personality that springs forth in every conversation. Don't hide your personality; just learn to share it in easy-to-swallow doses. Your prospects will appreciate your liveliness even more.

These are just some of the reasons salespeople tend to talk too much. Other reasons people talk too much could be that they don't like silence, they feel the need to preempt many perceived objections, or they tend to ramble.

The key is to understand why you, specifically, talk too much. That way you can develop a plan to cut down on the soliloquies.

What We Miss When We Talk

You may be thinking, "So what if I talk too much? I am, after all, very good at what I do and I know what I'm talking about. Isn't it important for my prospects and customers to know what I know so they can understand what I can do for them?" Perhaps, but you can miss a lot when you do too much of the talking, including the opportunity to build rapport and trust.

Buyers don't just buy your products and services. They buy a trusted advisor relationship. If you are doing all the talking, you will not pick up on the signals that indicate what in a relationship, besides your expertise and what you offer, is important to your customer. You miss the connection— the rapport that you need to build.

> It was impossible to get a conversation going, everybody was talking too much.
>
> —Yogi Berra

Plus, everyone loves to talk about themselves, to tell their story. If you do not give prospects a chance to do so, they often feel ignored, overwhelmed, and most important, unheard. This is not a good way to start relationships.

If you're talking too much, you miss the opportunity to uncover needs. When salespeople kick off sales conversations, many have strong knowledge of what they can do for customers, but understandably only a vague notion of what the prospects truly need. If you are doing all the talking, you can only guess which components of your solution set will offer the greatest value for the customer. Even if you have a clear notion of what clients need, until they express it to you, they won't know that, and they won't feel like they're going to be listened to *in the future*.

Don't discount that for many buyers their need to be listened to can feel as strong to them as whatever they need to purchase from you. Don't listen and you miss the chance to craft something special just for them. If you don't uncover all the needs, you miss out on building larger solutions (and generating the most revenue possible).

You also miss the chance to demonstrate what it is like to work with you. When you listen, show interest in customers' issues and ask insightful questions—you'll provide prospects with a glimpse at the real you.

Advocacy—The Yin to Inquiry's Yang

"If you want to demonstrate your expertise, if you want to build trust, ask a lot of good questions."

"You were given two ears and one mouth for a reason. Listen twice as much as you speak."

"Throwing ideas against the wall and seeing if something sticks . . . that's what amateurs do."

However you want to put it, the advice to "ask a lot of questions and wait before you put forth ideas" is often given to people new to sales.

Is it a bad piece of advice? No. Inquiry is a necessary part of any sales process. You want to engage in a dialogue, and questions are great because they can demonstrate that you:

- Understand the buyer's industry.
- Understand the buyer's situation, indicating that you "get" what they're going through.
- Have done homework on the buyer's company, and thus understand their organization.
- Can get the buyer thinking about topics essential to their success that they haven't yet considered, showing your insight and forethought.

However, asking questions alone won't win you deals. You need to capture attention, develop interest, and inspire action. In the name of asking the right questions you can get caught up in thinking that you need to ask questions incessantly to prove you're a good fit, valuable asset, and engaged listener.

Although buyers value sellers who listen, they are not interested in a pseudo-psychology session where they yammer on for 75 minutes while you ask questions, listen, and take notes, all while thoughtfully nodding your head and saying, "hmmmm." You can prove that you're a listener by simply listening at the appropriate times, confirming what you hear, and summarizing when helpful. Volume listening on your part and long periods of talking on their part can frustrate clients.

Advocacy is essential to sales success.

Power in Advocacy

Advocacy—the part where you set the agenda, educate, recommend, promote, and persuade—is just as important to the sales conversation as inquiry. Don't let anyone tell you differently.

Used correctly, advocacy will help you establish:

- *Capability.* Buyers must jump two hurdles when choosing to work with you. First, they must determine if you are a good general fit for their company and for their needs. This is commonly referred to as the *consideration* phase. Second follows the *selection* phase, the part that includes needs assessment, solution crafting, and choosing a provider.

  In both cases, buyers need to know what you do! It's especially important early on. Buyers ask themselves, "Who can help our company solve a problem like the one we have?" If they don't know what you do and the problems you solve, then you can't get in the game. No seat at the table. No at-bat, no home run.

Don't assume that buyers read your product and service descriptions, case studies, and the intellectual capital on your web site. Even if they've read it all and know what you do, many clients still need to hear it in your words, from your mouth, at a live meeting. Fail to share your capabilities or advocate for your particular offerings and you'll miss opportunities.

- *Credibility.* Asking questions isn't the only way to demonstrate credibility. Sharing a story about how you solved a problem in the past, describing how a customer's situation matches a dynamic you've seen a number of times, and sharing parts of your background and accomplishments also establishes credibility.

  Again, don't assume someone knows about you and all that you've done.

- *The big picture.* Don't underestimate how smart some buyers are. Although some babes in the decision-maker woods are truly lost, many buyers are just waiting for you to paint for them the picture of what's possible if they choose to work with you. Many buyers want to hear about your core products and services, how you typically apply them, and how they all work together.

  These systems thinkers want to know the big picture of what you do so they can file away in their brains where to apply your capabilities and assets at the time they need them. It's enough for some buyers to have you show them the complete landscape of what's possible. They will often take it from there.

  If you fail to give people the big-picture story—often in more detail than some sales pundits advise you to do—you can leave buyers confused as to how to plug you in, and leave you missing out on challenges they would have tapped you to solve.

  Naysayers will call this the "spray-and-pray approach." Sometimes prayers get answered.

- *The agenda:* All business leaders have an agenda—where they're taking their companies, their divisions, and their careers. As confident as many leaders seem, most yearn for trusted advisors to help them see a vision and set a direction.

A few simple words, "Here's how I recommend you move forward," are among the most powerful words in your vocabulary as an advisor. Some would say that this is too presumptuous, that leaders need us to help them find their own paths to success, that the danger in being wrong is just too high.

Nonsense! Decision makers want competent people to help them set an agenda they can believe in. Is there some risk involved? Of course. Welcome to sales.

Buyers don't always need to be taught to fish; sometimes they just need the right answers and confirmation that what they're thinking makes sense. Provide buyers direction and they'll value you highly.

- *Inspiration:* Decision makers are looking for fresh ideas and elegant ways to solve problems. Salespeople who get results have solution processes to share, passion to stimulate, and inspiration to trigger. When you show people what's possible by sharing your ideas, telling stories, and putting stakes in the ground, you can inspire buyers while at the same time you can shape the solution and make yourself the front-runner.

Your advocacy can start people on journeys down new and fruitful paths—paths that include working with you.

Guidelines for Balancing Advocacy and Inquiry

If you would like to find the right balance between talking too much and asking too many questions, what do you do next?

- *Approach business development conversations like client conversations:* Before you engage a business development conversation, think to yourself, "If this were a client meeting, and I was implementing our solution, helping them to get the most out of it, or solving a problem, how would I approach it?"

  If you approach the conversation this way instead of thinking, "I am now selling a new customer," it will help the conversation move along more naturally, keep you from talking too much, and help you to avoid sounding too self-interested.
- ***Think*** *about balancing advocacy and inquiry:* One person who worked with our company was thoughtful, hard working, and capable.

She wasn't, however, taken as seriously as she should have been taken by people who didn't know her because, when they met her, they were distracted by a verbal tick. She used to say "like" like way too often. When we pointed it out and said, "Just keep it in mind, listen for it, and work to minimize it," it disappeared within a month.

Advocacy and inquiry work the same way. If you keep this in your mind, you'll start to recognize when to use advocacy versus inquiry.

- *Ask open-ended questions:* If your goal is to get the client to start talking, ask open-ended questions. You'll be surprised at how much you will find out, how much it will help you generate more business, and how much it will help you be viewed as the best provider for them.

- *Practice your conversations:* We heard recently from a participant in a RAIN Selling seminar, "I hate role playing, but it was helpful and useful." Find a way to practice and you'll find yourself talking and listening the right amount.

As the old story goes:

Visitor to New York, asking a native New Yorker on the streets: "How do you get to Carnegie Hall?"

New Yorker: "Practice."

- *Tell stories:* The story is a very powerful tool in your advocacy tool kit. Stories allow you to demonstrate your grasp of the situation, advocate without directly pitching, and demonstrate your credibility.

Stories also allow you to capture the imagination of decision makers and bring them on an emotional journey. When you're telling stories, buyers are imagining the possibilities and building desire as they see themselves having the successes (and avoiding the failures) that you're sharing with them. Learn to tell good stories and you will inspire your prospects to want to be the hero in the next story.

I think generally, I do a good job when I tell a story about a similar situation and what I did to resolve the issue. If I can give a story that's similar to what they're trying to do and directly relates to my experience, I think that's really powerful in helping me gain the client.

—John Colucci, Attorney and Partner, McLane, Graf, Raulerson & Middleton, PA

- *Seek coaching:* Many salespeople can point to a time when a more experienced salesperson, after watching them lead a sales conversation, gave a piece of advice that made a significant difference in their conversation approach and success. Seek out this kind of coaching. Either from someone at your company or externally, the right feedback can help you win more customers and sell larger solution sets, often immediately.

When You Inquire, Listen to What the Prospect Says

In *How Clients Buy,*[2] 42 percent of those surveyed reported encountering potential providers that did not listen to them when the providers were selling.

Active listening is perhaps one of the most important characteristics a rainmaker can exhibit. Active listening is an essential component that will help you:

- Establish real rapport by demonstrating sincerity—don't listen and your potential client won't feel connected to you (and he shouldn't).
- Understand aspirations and afflictions—don't listen and you won't be able to help your client solve problems and create a new future.
- Ask the questions that will help prospects reach their goals.
- Give the best pieces of data and advice to help clients move forward and solve problems.
- Sense the prospect's underlying needs and concerns by hearing what he's really saying and perceiving his body language.
- Bring latent needs and concerns to the surface.

Often the technical training and development of sellers of complex products and services hinders their ability to be good listeners. If this is you, due to the nature of your work, you know a lot. This often causes sellers to err on the side of advocacy versus inquiry.

---

[2] RainToday.com, *How Clients Buy: 2009 Benchmark Report on Professional Services Marketing and Selling from the Client Perspective* (RainToday, 2009).

Develop Active Listening Skills

Consider the following five points to help you develop active listening skills:

1. *Plan to listen*: Once your chance to listen is gone, it's gone. There's no DVR rewind button for a live conversation. Before you enter any rainmaking conversation you should remind yourself to listen. Until it comes naturally every time, make listening a planned goal. After the meeting, ask yourself how well you did.

2. *Watch your talking*: If you're in play mode, you're not in record mode. If you find yourself talking too much, take a breather and start listening. Remember, if you are at lunch and you still have a full plate when the prospect is finished eating, you were talking too much.

3. *Paraphrase*: "Just so I understand" are four words that can serve you well. When someone else is describing something to you, they can take a long time to make relatively few points. When they're done, you can say, "Just so I understand, it seems that A and B are happening, and that's creating the problems of. . . . Is that correct?"

   When you rephrase a 10-minute explanation into 30 seconds of summary, prospects are impressed, partly by how smart you are (and you didn't even say much), but mostly by how well you listened.

4. *Explore*: After you paraphrase what your partner-in-conversation has said, asking follow-up questions becomes much easier. For example, you might open with the sentence noted above, "Just so I understand, it seems that A and B are happening, and that's creating the problems of. . . . Is that correct?"

   You can continue with an:

   - Aspiration question, "If that's the case, where do you think you could get if you were to add new capabilities in the operations areas?"
   - Affliction question, "With all that is happening, is that causing a lot of downtime for your staff?"
   - Impact question, "Really? How many hours per month do you think each person is losing?"

5. *Concentrate!* Seirenkai karate and jujitsu master Daniel Cohen is one of the most perceptive people we have ever met. From 50 feet away,

he can sense the best way to help someone improve their martial arts skills or learn a new technique. Sometimes he asks questions, sometimes he makes adjustments, and, every once in a while, he will just yell out "Concentrate!" And we can tell you, it's an attention getter.

Sometimes you don't need a tip or technique to help you get better at something, you simply need to break out of your pattern and apply a bit more intensity. If you find active listening difficult (or you are simply not listening), go past *active* and force yourself to listen *intensely*. Dare we say, "Concentrate!"

The more you ask questions and listen to prospects, the more you can figure out how best to help them. Make sure when you inquire, you listen to what the prospect says.

The more prospects know about us, the more they can see how they might apply what we do and how we can be a part of the solution-crafting process. And the more familiar they are with you, the more likely they are to have an affinity for you. Make sure you advocate, inspire, share, and set the agenda.

Advocacy and inquiry help us create deeper and more trusting relationships with prospects. Balancing advocacy and inquiry is not just good etiquette; it's good selling.

10 | Digging Deep into Needs

The Five Whys

In your needs discovery you should dig beneath the surface to understand the root causes of buyers' challenges. The Five Whys will help.

Popularized by Taiichi Ohno, one of the fathers of lean manufacturing, the Five Whys is a root-cause analysis technique that moves business leaders past putting Band-Aids on the symptoms of a problem, and instead helps them address the underlying causes, thus permanently solving the problem and creating a lasting new reality. The Five Whys help you work with prospects to uncover the root causes of what is driving their needs, and craft the most compelling, powerful, and lasting solutions.

Essentially, the Five Whys is to problem solving and critical thinking what removing weeds at the root is to gardening. Fix a symptom in business but not the underlying cause, and, much like a pulled weed with the root left in the ground, the symptom is bound to sprout up again. Fix the underlying cause of a problem at the root, and you will see lasting improvement.

Example Problem: The Production Line Stopped Again

- Why (1) did the production line stop? Answer: We blew a fuse.
- Why (2) did we blow a fuse? Answer: Because the bearings overheated.
- Why (3) did the bearings overheat? Answer: Because there is insufficient lubrication on them.
- Why (4) is there insufficient lubrication on the bearings? Answer: Because nobody oiled them.
- Why (5) did nobody oil them? Answer: Because we don't have a preventative maintenance schedule.
- Why (6) don't we have a preventative maintenance schedule? Answer: Silence.

Yes, this example has six Whys. You'll often find that it takes more than five Whys to discover the root of the problem. Five gives you the idea, but you should ask as many Whys as you need.

The idea is that once you get to silence, you are close to uncovering a root cause. The temptation for managers—who always have more to do than time to do it—is to try to solve the problem the moment they see a symptom they can tackle. In our scenario earlier, the plant manager might have ordered a fan be pointed at the bearings, keeping them at a cooler temperature and lessening the overheating problem. Or, someone might just switch the fuse, and then be ready to switch it again and again and again. Regardless, they wouldn't get the permanent fix.

The temptation for salespeople—who are often too eager to make a sale—is to stop at the first need they uncover where they can help. Rainmakers who are capable of getting to the bottom of things create stronger relationships, stronger foundations of trust, are seen as problem solvers and change agents, keep the competition closed out, and keep selling to clients year after year.

Here's how you might approach the Five Whys in a sales conversation:

> Prospect: "We need more training for our IT staff because we're receiving too many complaints about bad service."
> You: "Why are you receiving too many complaints about your service?" (Why 1)

Prospect: "Because response times are slow."

You: "Why are response times slow?" (Why 2)

Prospect: "Because our staff always seems backed up, no matter what we do."

You: "Why is the staff always backed up?" (Why 3)

Prospect: "Because requests come in that are deemed *urgent* that really aren't, and the ones that are urgent don't get immediate response. So we're always reacting like crazy every minute of the day."

You: "Why can't you differentiate between the really urgent problems and the not-so-urgent problems?" (Why 4)

Prospect: "Because we don't have definitions of what constitutes urgent, and we don't have a sufficient job ticket management system to help us keep it straight if we did."

You: "Why don't you have a job ticket management system that can help you keep it all sorted out?" (Why 5)

Prospect: "Because we looked at this two years ago and we didn't need it, but now we're twice the size and have so much more volume. No one's brought it up again with Jane, our COO, who makes the decisions about these kinds of things."

You: "Why hasn't anyone brought it up with Jane?" (Why 6)

Prospect: Silence.

You: "Is training for the IT staff what you need, or should you re-engage Jane about how a job ticket management system will improve response times and reduce complaints?"

Prospect: "Time to talk to Jane."

You: "Then you need to get approval, and install the job ticket management system?"

Prospect: "Right again."

You: "Let's talk about what you need in a job ticket management system, then. We see three options. One is right, depending on a few factors. Let's have a look."

Too many salespeople stop after Why 1. After all, you've uncovered a need and have a solution that can solve it. However, the solution results in the IT staff working harder and longer, becoming bitter, and starting to turn over. And the complaints keep coming. Some salespeople stop after

Why 2 and conclude that the solution is for their prospect to hire more IT people to handle the volume. Shortly thereafter, the complaints keep coming while labor cost rises.

If you stop too early, you, too, will find yourself helping the client solve the symptom of the problem and not the cause, not doing as well by your client as you should. It's by continuing to dig into what is really needed and why that gets you past "vendor" status and leads you toward "trusted advisor" status.

Trusted advisors help the most. They sell a lot, too.

Five Whys in Action

This story was relayed to us by a good friend at a large training and consulting firm:

"It was a $995 workshop for two days. And she was ready to give me a credit card number. I said, 'I'll be happy to put you in the workshop, but I would really like to understand more about what you would like to be able to do when you leave this class?'" (Why do you want to take this class?—Why 1)

Her response, "I want to learn how to build a leadership competency model for my organization."

"Can you tell me a little bit more of what you plan to do with the competency model once you build it?" (Why do you need to learn to build a competency model?—Why 2)

"I am in the process of building a leadership model and leadership programs for the entire United Nations secretariat."

"That's great. What kind of outcomes do you hope to achieve?" (Why are you going through the process?—Why 3)

"I want to tie a leadership skills model in with all of the changes that Kofi Anan is pursuing . . . building skills for all of the top leadership globally for the United Nations."

"I think this is a good workshop, but I can't guarantee that after two days, since you're new to this particular area, that you're going to have everything you need to go do that work. So here's what I'm asking. I'm going to send you to that workshop for free, but I'd also like you to have a conversation with one of our leading consultants on competency models."

To us: "That turned into my first consulting sale in 1998. I am now in my thirteenth year working with the United Nations."

—Dan Cohen, Regional Director, Linkage, Inc.

When using the Five Whys in your sales conversations, keep the following in mind:

- **Get agreement on the desired outcome.** Lack of agreement on the desired outcome happens often. Make sure you come to unambiguous agreement on the New Reality you are trying to create. Doing this will help you uncover the right need, position yourself as an integral part of the customer's success, and demonstrate your value as a partner regardless of what you might be selling.
- **Involve the right team.** Make sure you have the right buyers and sellers in the room that will help get to the root cause. If the discussion starts off with "We need a new server," you need to have the technical experts (yours and theirs) available who know what may be driving the surface need for a new server, and what putting in a new server will affect. The blind leading the blind makes for a lot of expensive walks into brick walls.
- **Employ good logic.** Don't make specious cause/effect conclusions. Like a geometry proof gone awry, make one mistake in the middle and you can find yourself on the wrong path for the duration. A marketing leader once told me (Mike) that because their direct mail campaigns didn't work, direct mail doesn't work. I told him that I once tried to bake a cake but it didn't rise. My conclusion: Cakes don't rise. Imagine my surprise when I learned that cakes do indeed rise, I just didn't know how to bake. In the same vein, not everyone knows how to run a direct mail campaign.
- **Allow leeway to people as they try to answer, "Why?"** You will often find a number of possible root causes and solutions. You might not know definitely the answer to why at first. Take care not to shoot early ideas down. The idea is not to answer the Five Whys in five minutes, but to answer them correctly in the appropriate amount of time.

- **Keep asking "Why?" until you get to the real need.** If you come up with a number of possible answers to the first Why question, you may find yourself asking more than five additional Whys. It is also common that there is more than one root problem. In this case, focus on one sequence of Whys at a time.
- **Determine which Whys to confirm.** As you go through the possible answers to the Why questions, you might find that some seem more plausible than others. Remove any Why answers you know aren't worth investigating, and discuss which possibilities you should continue to investigate and confirm.
- **Realize you might need a bigger process to uncover the root.** In some cases, you might find that answering Why requires further analysis. For example:
  - We need to change our compensation plan.
  - Why do you say you need a new compensation plan? (Why 1)
  - We have high turnover.
  - Why do you think you have high turnover? (Why 2)
  - Employees aren't satisfied with their jobs.
  - What evidence do you see of that? (Why 3)
  - Because they've been telling us more and more, and they tell us on the way out.
  - Do you know for certain why they're not satisfied? That compensation is the key issue? (Why 4)
  - Answer: Silence

Before you solve the turnover issue you need to find out the answer to Why in a more rigorous way than just brainstorming. You may find the decision makers start arguing about why there's high turnover. Some think low pay, thus the compensation *need* mentioned first. Some think it is bad hiring practices. Some think it is bad management. Others think it's just too frustrating to work at the company. The compensation issue suddenly becomes one of a sea of possibilities.

If you can't figure out Why through your sales conversations, your next step can be to offer a robust analysis of Why. An up-front analysis or assessment is often the first step in many companies' sets of offerings. After the analysis you can recommend solutions with the confidence that will address the root need, in this case, whatever is causing dissatisfied employees.

"First Why Question" Starter Ideas

- "You tried something similar in the past, but it didn't work. Why did that happen?"
- "You've had this as a priority for a while, but haven't acted on it. Why is that?"
- "So you've mentioned that the problem is affecting your ability to compete in global markets. Why do you think that's happening?"
- "What are you looking to get done . . . why are we here?"
- "It seems that everything is in place to move forward, but the process has stalled. Why aren't things moving along?"
- "I get the feeling that the three of you aren't on the same page. Is that true? Why?"

Going through the process of asking the Five Whys positions you as a trusted advisor, demonstrates your expertise in solving problems, builds your credibility, and differentiates you. Not to mention that the sellers who master this technique often sell a much broader solution set.

If you employ the Five Whys, you'll know that as you uncover needs and craft solutions, you're addressing the root cause, and you will fix the real problem—for good—while your competitors are only offering Band-Aids.

11

16 Principles of Influence in Sales

Let no man imagine that he has no influence. Whoever he may be, and wherever he may be placed, the man who thinks becomes a light and a power.

—Henry George

Have you ever wanted something so badly you could barely think of anything else?

You wouldn't be satisfied until you had it. And you would have done anything to get it.

It's unlikely that you randomly woke up one sunny morning, got hit with Cupid's arrow, and started feeling like this. Whether conscious of it or not, you took a journey from not even being aware of your future object of desire, to yearning, pining, and longing to have it.

As sellers, it's up to us to create the yearn and pine, and help buyers make decisions to satisfy their needs to have it . . . by, of course, buying from you.

Throughout *Rainmaking Conversations*, we've shared with you the RAIN Selling framework—a framework that will help you learn *how* to sell like a rainmaker. We haven't, though, spent much time talking about *why* it all works.

Before we get started, know this: Until you intend to influence, you won't. Much like becoming a rainmaker, becoming a master influencer takes focus and intent, two things that, when it comes to influence, many salespeople don't have. One salesperson said to us, "Buyers know what they want. Far be it for me to interject what I think is right. It's my job to help them succeed with what they decide, not to influence the decision."

This person never sold much.

Accept your role as an influencer if you don't want to match their results. Bring buyers down a path of your choosing and help them make a decision in your favor. Take control of the buying process.

Take care, however, not to confuse control with coercion. In sales, your control should be subtle: Lead the conversation down the right path by asking questions, setting agendas by sharing ideas, summarizing and communicating the impact of taking a course of action, involving the prospect in creating solutions, and recommending action. If you try to control with an iron fist you will create more resistance than partnership.

Coercion won't get you far, but the 16 Principles of Influence in Sales will serve you well.

Principle 1. Attention

Like drivers zooming down the highway, most prospects are going at 90 miles an hour to wherever they're headed. Good luck to anyone who gets in their way, tries to flag them down, or tries to change their course.

In spite of this, you need to get their attention. In our chapter on communicating your value proposition, we described the tried and true AIDA framework. AIDA starts with attention. So must you. Until you get their attention, they will continue zooming by you at 90 miles per hour.

What it is: Draw focus away from other things and toward you.
Why it works: Attention is your ante to get and stay at the table. If you're not
   at the table, you can't influence.
How rainmakers apply it:

- Be memorable when prospecting and in your sales conversations.
- Highlight differentiation.
- Employ attention-grabbing marketing activities like delivering speeches, sending stellar direct mail pieces, running seminars, writing

books and articles, and leveraging online marketing like blogging and search-engine marketing.

- Build a strong brand reputation.
- Work networking events and relationships with energy and conversation savvy.

Takeaway: Capture the attention of busy prospects.

Principle 2. Curiosity

Once you have someone's attention, the easiest thing to do is to lose it.

Your goal is to pique the prospect's curiosity. Curiosity is a powerful concept. People know what they have, but they want to know what they're *missing.* Give them the sense that they might be missing something, and they'll naturally want to know more.

At this stage, resist the temptation to sell the full solution. You're not yet trying to close. You're trying to open—open minds, open a relationship, and open a window to keep going.

Once you divert prospective buyers' attention toward you, gravity is pulling it back to wherever it was before. Your charge is to convert the initial attention into interest in seeking new information. If you want to keep their interest, their curiosity must be more powerful than the forces drawing them back to their 90 mile an hour journey to someplace else.

What it is: After you get attention, keep attention by fueling their desire to learn more.

Why it works: People have a need to know what they're missing. They want to know what else is out there. Once they have curiosity, they'll want to satisfy it.

How rainmakers apply it:

- Focus prospecting on the value of speaking with you, not just in your ultimate offering.
- Help them see their value gap, and let them know you can help close it.
- Highlight differentiation.
- Entice with possibilities (e.g., increase productivity, faster time to market).

- Build desire for the answer (e.g., "4 Secrets of Innovative Companies," what our benchmark research showed, the top trend in the next wave of data storage).

Takeaway: Pique curiosity to keep attention.

Principle 3. Desire

Desire is the gap between where someone is and where he wants to be.

This is where the two buyer mind-sets—problem solving and future seeking—come into play. The more you can stoke someone's desire to change his reality, the more you'll be able to influence him.

We're Happy Now: Prospects will sometimes say, "We're happy with where we are." They might well be, but this is often because they don't know about the possibility of improvement yet. If you can communicate the possibility and the path to get there, they might find they're not as happy as they thought they were.

In business, the gap between where they are now and the new reality is typically communicated in return-on-investment terms. When buyers start to see what's in it for them, this value stokes emotions.

First among them: desire.

What it is: The gap between where people are and where they want to be.
Why it works: Desire creates dissatisfaction. Dissatisfaction (a.k.a. wants and needs) is the impetus for action in sales.
How rainmakers apply it:

- Uncover explicit needs—needs they know they have.
- Uncover latent needs—needs hidden beneath the surface.
- Share examples of the possibilities in the form of case studies, testimonials, white papers, research, presentations, and demonstrations.
- Open buyers' eyes to the new reality.

Takeaway: Stoke desire by helping prospects see the possibility of being someplace better.

Principle 4. Envy

Desire is powerful. Envy is desire with a turbo boost.

If your prospects want something they don't have, their desires will drive them. If they want something that *other people have*, their unhappiness will eat away at them until they get it. The unhappier they are with their current situations compared to what's possible, the more likely they will be to act.

There's nothing wrong with pointing out to the CEO of a $10 million business that his business should be a $20 million business, and you know how to help get there. And there's nothing wrong with giving him the sense of what it will feel like to run (and then sell, exceeding his personal financial goals) that $20 million business by showing him how others have done it.

If he is happy with the $10 million he'll accept the status quo. But if he wants the $20 million and other people just like him have it, his impetus to act will grow.

What it is: The desire for what other people have.
Why it works: When other people have something, a person thinks, "I should
     have that," and "Why don't I have that?" These thoughts amplify desire.
How rainmakers apply it: Share examples of how you've helped other people
     in the same situation accomplish the success, reach the goal, or acquire
     the position the person wants for himself.
Takeaway: Envy turbo charges desire.

Principle 5. Emotional Journey

In the preface to *Lyrical Ballads,* William Wordsworth wrote, "I have said that poetry is the spontaneous overflow of powerful feelings: it takes its origin from emotion recollected in tranquillity: the emotion is contemplated till, by a species of reaction, the tranquillity gradually disappears, and an emotion, kindred to that which was before the subject of contemplation, is gradually produced, and does itself actually exist in the mind."[1]

---

[1] William Wordsworth, *Lyrical Ballads, With Other Poems* (1800), online at: www
     .gutenberg.org/cache/epub/8905/pg8905.html.

In other words, it's the poet's job to produce a predetermined feeling in the reader. If someone sits down to read some poetry, if the poet did his job, the reader will feel the emotion. In essence, the poet takes the reader on an emotional journey.

Successful salespeople do the same, especially through storytelling. When listening to a story, people put themselves in the *diegesis*, the world of the story. Worry, fear, anger, worthlessness, love, acceptance, success, anticipation, validation, regret, victory, and freedom are all emotions great storytellers elicit as a matter of course. Not only do people feel these emotions when listening to a story, they see the images in their minds. When connected to powerful emotions, these images will stick with them.

When sellers tell stories, they take the buyer on an emotional journey so the buyer doesn't just *know* where they want to be, they *feel* it and *see* it. And if the feeling is different and better from how they feel now, they'll be compelled to do something about it.

What it is: Eliciting and developing lasting images and feelings.
Why it works: People forget what they heard and remember how they felt.
How rainmakers apply it:

- Build strong connections and relationships.
- Build emotion in all stages of RAIN.
- Show possibilities through social proof to stoke desire, belief, and envy.
- Tell stories to create lasting images and feelings.

Takeaway: Take your buyers on an emotional journey.

Principle 6. Belief

Imagine the effect on your ability to influence when your buyer thinks any one of the following about what you're proposing to do:

- "This won't work."
- "This has the possibility of working, but could also fail on so many levels."
- "This might work."

- "This should work."
- "This will work."
- "This is a complete no-brainer. There's no way it won't work."

You'll have maximum ability to influence when prospects:

- Believe their situation should be different—the possibility of better is real.
- Believe they can do something about it—they don't feel like they are at the mercy of circumstance.
- Believe in the path to the change—what you've shared with them *will* work.

The concepts of substantiation and trust in RAIN Selling work closely with belief. Substantiation helps someone believe something is going to work (i.e., it's worked for someone else . . . the logic is impeccable). Trust removes skepticism and increases faith in you.

What it is: Confidence in the efficacy of people, process, company, product, or service.

Why it works: People avoid risk. The more they believe, the less risk they perceive, the more action they take.

How rainmakers apply it:

- Consistency in behavior (i.e., you do what you say you're going to do and they start to believe you. By proxy, they place more faith in your offerings).
- Leverage of brand, history of excellence, history of success.
- Demonstrations.
- Social proof—case studies, testimonials, references.

Takeaway: Increase belief. Reduce risk. Inspire action.

Principle 7. Justification

People buy with their hearts and justify with their heads. Even if you are able to capture the hearts of your buyers, if you can't make the ROI case for working with you, you won't make the sale. ROI and emotion are tied closely together. For example:

ROI	Emotion
I'll double my income . . .	. . . so I'll be *happy.*
We'll increase our margins by 3 percent . . .	. . . I'll be promoted to vice president and won't have to *worry* anymore about *feeling accepted.* And my wife and son will be *proud* of me.
My assets will rise, and I'll retire with the financial cushion I need . . .	. . . so I'll finally be *secure* and *free.*
We'll save money and won't have to hire a full time IT director . . .	. . . and I won't be *frustrated* for four months with trying to hire another person like our last joker, while everyone complains to me in the meantime.

The promise of ROI is the reason why prospects should listen to you . . . meet with you . . . gather the decision makers . . . request a proposal . . . and buy.

In the end, they may buy because they like you best, because they want to be able to relax on their weekends instead of worrying about what they worry about, or they'll have less frustration at the office. Perhaps they'll buy because they believe it's the right thing to do. These are emotional needs, but these emotional needs must be justified with a rational case.

What it is: The rational argument that supports why they should buy.
Why it works: Belief in ROI ⇨ Emotional Needs ⇨ Desire to Buy ⇨ Need
    to *justify purchase rationally* to self and others
How rainmakers apply it:

- ROI arguments at various stages of the sales cycle.
- Development and connection of ROI to emotions.
- Superior development of impact and delivery of New Reality with all three value bases covered (resonate, differentiate, and substantiate).

Takeaway: Buyers need to justify their purchases. Even if emotions are present, "because I want it" isn't good enough beyond impulse buys. No justification in a complex sale, no purchase.

Principle 8. Trust

Near the end of *Indiana Jones and the Last Crusade,* Indy is faced with an impossible task: Walk on air over a seemingly endless chasm, or plunge to his demise. He takes a tentative step and, to his surprise, no plunging. No demising.

He makes a leap of faith and he doesn't fall.

The principle of trust works closely with the principle of belief. Belief is faith that something will *work,* trust is faith in *you.* If you have ever tried to buy something you believed would be excellent, and had to deal with the hassle of buying it despite your doubt about the motives and the competence of the salesperson, you know the difference.

When someone chooses to work with you, they'll need to satisfy the following four areas:

- *Competence:* Do you know what you're talking about and can you actually help? They're looking to trust that you and your offerings are capable and credible.
- *Reliability:* Will you do what you say you will do? They're looking to trust that they can rely on you to deliver on your promises.
- *Risk:* Is it safe? If I take this leap of faith with you, will I fall? They're looking to reduce the risk of failure.
- *Self-Interest:* Will you take advantage of me if it suits your interests? They're looking to trust that you'll be a good steward of their vulnerability.

What it is: Belief is faith that something will *work.* Trust is faith in *you.*
Why it works: Trust is the foundation of the sale. No trust, no sale.
How rainmakers apply it:

- Play to win-win (Rainmaker Principle 1).
- Never compromise integrity.
- Make your motives transparent.
- Do what you say you're going to do in the sales process.
- Apply substantiation message strategies.

Takeaway: Trust is the foundation of rainmaking success.

Principle 9. Stepping Stones

Once people get on a path, they're much more likely to stay on that path. People are driven to be consistent.

This is borne out in sales and marketing all the time. Getting someone to take a first meeting with you can be a challenge. You have to talk to many people to generate precious few first meetings. Getting a second meeting is much easier. If someone reads a white paper or watches a webinar, they're more likely to accept an initial meeting than those who don't. If someone buys something once, even in a small amount, they're more likely to buy it again and buy more of it.

The more people are familiar with something, the more likely they are to like it and trust it. People are even willing to invest money in something familiar while actually ignoring logical investment practices.[2] You can become familiar to people by starting small and working your way to something big.

What it is: Start people on the path to interacting with you and they're more likely to continue in the future.

Why it works: People are driven to be consistent. Ask them to do something once and they're more likely to continue to do it and be open to expanding sizes and scopes.

How rainmakers apply it:

- *Domino strategy:* Provide offers that pique curiosity. Satisfy that curiosity, then present a new curiosity immediately after. For example, you invite prospects to a seminar to learn the four keys to break through [anything]. At the seminar, you introduce and explain the four keys. All the while, attendees are thinking, "How do we stack up?" At the end of the seminar, you introduce your assessment process to help them measure how they stack up. Now they want to know even more.
- *Layering strategy:* You start with a particular offer and, during the process of selling, implementing, or servicing the customer, you offer

---

[2]G. Huberman, "Familiarity breeds investment," *Journal of Review of Financial Studies*, vol. 14, no. 3.

additional capabilities to enhance his ROI or personal satisfaction. In other words, get started somewhere with the client, and then, when he trusts you and sees you are as good as he had hoped, you can cross-sell, up-sell, and deepen account penetration.

Offers—The First Dominos in the Series

Here is a list of common offers that you can use as the first domino in the series:

- White papers
- Enewsletter subscriptions
- Membership programs
- Books
- Seminars
- Conference presentations
- Webinars
- Podcasts
- Lunches
- One-on-one presentations
- Invitations to join you at events

Takeaway: Buying is a leap of faith. Shorten that leap of faith with stepping stones.

Principle 10. Ownership

Q. How many psychologists does it take to change a light bulb?
A. One, but the light bulb has to want to change.

Until an individual takes ownership over decisions, actions, and results, your ability to influence him or her is limited.

Imagine for a minute that you convince someone to take a course of action, but he is still skeptical. He says "Yes, let's do it. If you think it's going to work, then I'll give it a try," a few things can happen:

- The buyers do not devote themselves to the success of the process, the process fails, and you never sell to them again.
- They go back to their decision-maker colleagues who talk them out of it.
- They think better of it and in a few days renege, or get on to other things and decide there's no time for you.

If you want your sales to stick, you need buyers to believe *they* are responsible for their own decisions, that *their* urgency and analysis are driving the decision, and that *their* beliefs and needs will be validated by moving forward.

Like the light bulb, they need to want to change.

Imagine trying to force a person on your team to sell every day when she doesn't want to and doesn't believe it will work. She'll sell with no energy. No conviction. Take your eyes off this salesperson for a minute, and she'll start doing just about anything else.

Buying is similar. Until prospects themselves feel the need to change, believe they can change, and want to do the hard work of changing, they will inevitably fall back to their current state and current reality.

What it is: Assuming responsibility for making change happen.

Why it works: Ownership breeds investment in the process and a stake in the outcome. The stronger the sense of ownership, the more people will identify themselves with the success of the outcome. And the more they'll feel validated and accepted by others when the outcome happens.

How rainmakers apply it:

- Seek out, uncover, and enhance desire to change.
- Uncover aspirations, afflictions, and impact.
- Discover if the desire for the impact elicits a willingness to change.[3]
- Maximize involvement of the buyer in the buying and solution crafting processes.
- Maintain a peer relationship with buyers; apply the influence principle of indifference as warranted.

Takeaway: Until buyers take ownership, their commitment to act, if they have any at all, will be shallow and fleeting.

---

[3] A salesperson we knew made a compelling case to a CFO of a major hospital system that his product would save the buyer $10 million a year. He said, "I agree, but I'm not solving $10 million problems right now. I'm solving $50 million problems." His desire for the outcome wasn't strong enough to make a change.

Principle 11. Involvement

When you have a hand in creating something, you're more likely to be a passionate advocate for its success.

Lack of involvement breeds emotional disinterest. This isn't what you want. You want to feed desire, ownership, and belief. You want people personally and emotionally invested.

When people have a part in coming up with answers and actions themselves, they feel more ownership over them. Think about it: Can you tell someone about an epiphany you had, and then expect that person to feel the same, believe the same, and commit the same? Or do you need to help them realize their own epiphanies?

It's not just in the sales process that involvement breeds emotional investment. Salespeople who keep customers engaged postpurchase, who get buyers to use their solutions to the fullest, and who keep interacting with them and their companies keep them as customers longer. Absence does not make the heart grow fonder. Involvement does.

What it is: Getting buyers to become partners in the selling process.
Why it works: When people feel that they are involved, that they contribute, that they're listened to, and that they make an impact themselves, they become invested in the process and apply themselves to see it through.
How rainmakers apply it:

- Balance advocacy and inquiry to involve buyers in your discussions.
- Ask their opinions. Involve them in solution crafting.
- Have buyers accept responsibility for their part of the buying process.
- Have longer, involved working meetings with them in the various stages of the process.
- Use stepping stones:
  — Have buyers attend programs, read content, view presentations and webinars.
  — Offer trials, demonstrations, and the opportunity to interact with your offering before they buy it.

Takeaway: Involve prospects in the sale. Enlist their efforts in the process.

Principle 12. Desire for Inclusion

People will often say they are not influenced by other people's thinking, but they usually are. When you can say "25 percent of companies in the Fortune 500 use our technology," or "More than 400 companies have employed this approach successfully," or mention that other decision makers are doing something (e.g., attending the same training, using the same handheld device, embracing a certain management methodology), they are more inclined to do the same.

People don't want to be left out. They want to feel included.

This is why case studies, testimonials, references, and lists of prominent clients can work to your advantage. Social proof is a powerful concept. It influences the desire to be included, feeds envy, and is a key component of building belief and trust.

If you've ever wondered why infomercials include incessant testimonial stories, this is it. Those not keen on the concept of desire for inclusion might think, "One testimonial is enough, and three is the limit," but they'd be wrong. There's a cumulative, layering effect. The more you use social proof, the more you stoke the desire to be included. ("Look at how often it's worked!" "All these people can't be wrong." "If they can do it, I can do it.")

If you've ever seen a time-share sales pitch, you know that someone is going to get up publicly and commit to buy right when the pitchman is reaching his crescendo. But they're never alone. Another person gets up. And another. And another.

Is it real or is it artificial? We won't comment on that, but it is orchestrated. For good reason.

What it is: People want to feel included.

Why it works: Inclusion supports people's needs for validation. When they're on the outside, they're an island. When they're doing something others are doing, they're part of the pack . . . the team . . . the crew . . . the people in the know. If other people are doing something, it will increase envy and curiosity around what they might be missing.

How rainmakers apply it: Use social proof in all of its forms.

Takeaway: Stoke desire to be included.

Principle 13. Scarcity

- Buy now! Only three left.
- Register by October 17. After that, you can't sign up, and we're never running this event again.
- Without having seen the light of day in 127 years, these 2,000 gold coins from the U.S. Mint are extremely rare.

Scarcity is one of the most cited, most commonly employed, persuasion strategies. People value things that are rare and hard to get.

The key to using scarcity the right way is to combine it with trust. If scarcity is used improperly as a strategy, if you're not completely honest about it, if it's used as a trick, it will undermine trust. This is not something you want to do if repeat business, referrals, or reputation have any bearing on your success.

The two most common manifestations of scarcity is lack of availability and time. If something is rare, people simply want it more. If they think time or quantities will run out, they're more likely to act.

What it is: People value rarity, and don't want to miss out on opportunity.
Why it works: We'd like to pretend this is more complicated than it is, but scarcity works because . . . people value rarity, and don't want to miss out on opportunity.
How rainmakers apply it:

- Highlight differentiation.
- Highlight potential loss of opportunity if the buyer doesn't take action.
- Combine decision time with scarcity. When other factors like emotional journey, justification, ownership, and desire for inclusion combine with scarcity you maximize likelihood of action. When someone is ready to act but then doesn't, you encounter diminishing intent. If they don't buy when they're ready, the more time that passes, the less likely they will be to buy. Use scarcity to minimize the chance that time will drag out when a buyer is ready to make a decision.
- Make limited quantities available as a business strategy. Make quantities available only at certain times, and not always on the shelf.

Takeaway: People are attracted to rarity, and don't want to miss opportunities.

Principle 14. Likeability

You will need a pick and a harness to climb the mountain of research touting the influence benefits of likeability. Remember, however, that although you should be likeable, your desire to be liked should not overshadow your need to succeed in sales. If this happens, your need for approval will negatively affect your results.

What it is: Generating affinity for you and your offerings.

Why it works: Likeability creates and enhances opportunity for conversations at all stages. People pay attention to, talk to, and buy from people they like. They like to work with people they like. They want to see people they like succeed.

How rainmakers apply it: It's less that rainmakers apply being likeable, they just are likeable. Explore Chapter 5, Rapport, for ideas. If you feel you'd like to increase your likeability, read books like *The Power of Charm,*[4] *Trust Me: Four Steps to Authenticity and Charisma,*[5] and *The Likeability Factor.*[6]

Takeaway: People pay attention to, listen to, and buy from people they like.

Principle 15. Indifference

You want to be likeable, but you don't want to *need* to be liked, *need* to be accepted, and *need* to make a sale. The harder you push someone to accept your message, the more resistance you will meet to having it accepted. The needier you seem, the more buyers will discount you, look askance at your product and service, and doubt what you tell them. Neediness is repelling.

On the other hand, do not equate indifference with playing hard to get, being unresponsive, or seeming disengaged from the process. You can have passion about your products, services, and company. You can believe the merits for the prospect of moving forward. You can communicate those merits thoughtfully and energetically.

---

[4]Brian Tracy and Ron Arden, *The Power of Charm: How to Win Anyone Over in Any Situation* (AMACOM, 2006).

[5]Nick Morgan, *Trust Me: Four Steps to Authenticity and Charisma* (Jossey-Bass, 2008).

[6]Tim Sanders, *The Likeability Factor: How to Boost Your L-Factor and Achieve Your Life's Dreams* (Three Rivers Press, 2006).

But seem like you need to make the sale and the prospect will disengage. Desperation is not a good influence strategy.

The key is not trying to *seem* indifferent. Be indifferent. Be okay with not getting this deal. Be okay with moving on to other opportunities. Find out if the buyer is moving toward a no when you sense her backing off. You'll often find that when you inquire, you'll draw her back in. If they're truly not interested, you'll waste less time and can move on to find better prospects.

Employ Indifference by Reversing Direction

Reversing direction is a strategy that communicates and employs the concept of indifference. You can reverse direction:

- **Early in a conversation**
  "We've been talking for a while now and I'm not getting the sense that there's anything that's grabbing you. If you feel like you're getting everything you want out of the area of budgeting and financial control, and you don't feel the opportunity is here at all to make improvements, perhaps we should end the conversation now, and save the time for both of us." (Pause)

- **If you're not getting callbacks**
  (In a voicemail or customized e-mail) "Sarah, it's Jim Smith calling. Sorry we haven't been able to connect in the last several weeks. I know you were keen on moving forward with discussions around finding out which of your P&Ls are most profitable, and where you can improve profit overall, but I haven't heard back the last few times I've reached out. What's usually the case in these situations is that this isn't on your radar screen anymore and that you've moved on. If I don't hear back from you, I'll assume that's where we are. Meanwhile, I'm signing off for now and won't continue to reach out. However, if that's not the case, and something else is up, I'd look forward to continuing the conversation. If so, call me back."

What it is: Emotional detachment to the outcome of making the sale.

Why it works: Indifference affects two people: you and the buyer.

- When you are indifferent, you won't need the approval of the buyer to feel like you, yourself, are valuable. Thus, you won't fall into the conversation traps that beset salespeople with the need for approval, and you'll be able to focus on the business value you bring to the table.

- When buyers perceive your indifference, they won't feel strong-armed. This builds their ownership of the issue. Your indifference will support trust building because the buyer will perceive that you place your value on the offering and what it can do, not the sale itself. Indifference also supports likeability because buyers perceive a peer relationship, and because neediness, the opposite of indifference, is repelling.

How rainmakers apply it:

- Don't be needy personally. Work out issues you may have with need for approval.
- Don't be needy professionally. Always improve your pipeline and you won't be.
- Don't come across needy. Focus on value to the buyer, not your desire for the sale (Rainmaker Principle 4).
- Reverse direction as appropriate.

Takeaway: Be ready and willing to walk away, and happy to do it if the situation warrants.

Principle 16. Commitment

When people make written and public commitments, they're more likely to keep them.

When you get a yes, the commitment trifecta is to get the verbal yes in front of other people, get the yes in writing, and get the buyer to communicate publicly (such as an e-mail to the buyer's team or a press release) that they're moving forward with you.

Written and public commitments are stronger than verbal and private commitments. Stories of verbal yeses that disappear into the ether a week later litter the sales landscape. It's much rarer to find a buyer who backs away from the commitment after saying yes, signing an agreement, and stating publicly that they're moving forward.

What it is: Get verbal, written, and public commitment.

Why it works: People want to be trusted. They know that if they follow through on their commitments, people will respect their word. Written and public commitments increase the social pressure on a decision maker to appear that her commitment means something, and that she's not untrustworthy, scatterbrained, or a waffler.

How rainmakers apply it:

- Ask for commitment at the right time.
- Get signatures.
- Communicate commitments publicly.

Takeaway: Gain commitment, get it in writing, and make it public.

As you consider the 16 Principles of Influence, remember that you must influence the right people. If a prospect doesn't have the power to make or influence a decision to buy from you, there's no reason for you to influence that person.

But never think you don't have the power to influence. You do. Study influence. Think about how to apply it. Do so, and you'll become a light and a power in sales.

12

Tips for Leading Rainmaking Conversations

Whatever's undiscussable limits what's possible.

—Steve Williamson

Rainmaking conversations follow well-worn patterns, and satisfy the same conditions, regardless of the product or service you're selling. Up until now, we have covered a number of concepts in depth. In this chapter, you find a menu of tips, ideas, and examples that can help you succeed in each conversation stage.

As you read the suggestions and examples, use them as inspirational guidance, not verbatim instruction. Everyone has their own style and tone. Use yours. Meanwhile, the examples will give you the direction on what to get across and how you might approach doing so.

Before we dive in, note that the eight rainmaking conversation stages are not necessarily linear. They go somewhat in order, but you will usually move back and forth between various stages throughout your conversations.

Whatever's happening in the conversation, remember Rainmaker Principle 4—think buying first, selling second. It will help you keep everything in the proper perspective.

Your Selling Process	Their Buying Process
1. Rapport Building	First reaction—do I like this person?
2. Conversation kickoff	
• Conversation purpose and outcome	• Is this person:
• Value proposition for meeting and company	— Prepared?
	— Organized?
• Introductions	— Competent?
• Inquiry into meeting hopes	— Looking to listen as well as talk?
3a. Needs discovery— Interest and desire	
• Company overview	• Does this person:
• Background on the problem	— Understand my needs?
	— Understand my situation?
• Typical solutions positioned as failing reasons why it happens	— Make general sense?
	— Stand out from the crowd as a person? With his viewpoint? With his offerings and capabilities?
• New approach	
• Typical impact	
3b. Needs discovery— Aspirations and afflictions	• Am I willing to lift the veil on what's really going on here, and share our aspirations and afflictions?
• Customer needs profile— discover aspirations and afflictions	
• Summarize and confirm	
4. Impact analysis	
• Ask questions based on explicit and latent aspirations and afflictions	• Do I see the ROI?
	• How will this impact *me*?
	• Is solving this to-do list worthy?
• Outline typical impact— employ impact modeling	• Do I want to take this on now?
• Gain agreement on impact ranges	

Your Selling Process	Their Buying Process

5. New reality
- Describe possible new realities
- Set agenda for possible paths forward
- Involve buyer in new reality design and process to achieve

- Is their approach to solving the problem
  — Credible?
  — Desirable?
  — Different than the norm?
- Will this work here?

6. Determine buying process
- Discover interest levels
- Determine buying process and players
- Involve appropriate decision makers
- Determine F in FAINT

- Should I bring in the rest of the buying team?
- (If the buyer is not the top decision maker)
- Am I willing to risk introducing this person and process to them? Am I willing to share what our processes are?
- What else do I need to know or do to make a decision?

7. Next steps
- Confirm reasons to continue
- Suggest and calibrate next steps
- Gain agreement on the next step and when it will take place

- Am I willing to commit right now to moving this forward?
- Do I feel like I have a hand in how to shape the process?
- Am I being dealt with reasonably?

8. Postmeeting—After you leave
- Write confirmation document
- Prepare for next conversation

- Do I trust them?
- Do I need what they're selling?
- Is the solution a good one?
- Is there enough value for me to move it forward?

Stage 1. Rapport Building

- Attend to the basics. Say hello, maintain eye contact and deliver a firm, but not death-grip, handshake.
- Break the ice with small talk as appropriate. Be prepared to chat (some people prefer not to talk shop right away), and be prepared to fill time while you wait for everyone to show up.
- If the relationship and likeability are particularly important for your sale or buyer, don't rush past rapport.
- Lead the transition into the business at hand. Maintaining control of the conversation is crucial, and starts with your transitioning into the agenda for the discussion.

Stage 2. Meeting Kickoff

Depending on your goals for the meeting, you won't need to do everything in the table that follows. If it's a first meeting, you can follow the guidelines below to plan the meeting flow. Also, keep in mind how much time you have. For example, if the meeting is slated for 20 minutes, you may not have time for long introductions if there are five people in the room. Calibrate accordingly.

Topic	Examples
Meeting introduction You call the meeting to order, and set a clear direction	Thank you everyone for coming today. I'm glad you could all make it and I'm looking forward to having an interesting discussion with you.
Purpose of the meeting You set the overall premise of the meeting	**Example 1:** As we discussed on the telephone, we have just published research on the best practices in zero-based planning, and how it is affecting manufacturing firm profitability. Today, we're going to take about 20 minutes to walk through the core findings and then spend the rest of the time talking about the implications for you. We also want to give you all a

Topic	Examples
	chance to ask more questions about the research and our experience working with other companies on these challenges. **Example 2:** Jim and I discussed at our luncheon that you were dealing with three core challenges, including . . . Jim asked me to come in today to broaden the discussion with you all and to see if we can come up with some new ways to tackle the challenges. **Example 3:** As Alexis knows from attending our webinar, we've been able to help technology firms speed up their software engineering and development timeframe by between 20 percent and 50 percent with our CAD product. We're going to talk today about how we've been able to do it, and see if the conditions are such here that we might be able to speed up the same processes for you.
People and company introductions Everyone introduces themselves. You open the door to give the overview about your company. Take a few minutes to introduce yourself and your firm. You'll be able to introduce more of what you do during the conversation itself.	Before we get started, I'd like to take a few minutes to introduce myself and, as well, learn a little about you. [You introduce yourself, and give a brief company intro. Think value proposition positioning statement, not presentation.] [They introduce themselves.]

(continued)

Topic	Examples
Time frame You confirm (and sometimes set) the time frame for the meeting	We're scheduled for an hour (20 minutes, 30 minutes, 90 minutes) for this meeting. Before we get started, does this still work?
Agenda Your agenda—you already introduced the meeting purpose, but you can add anything else that you want to make sure you cover at the meeting Their agenda(s)—you ask them what would make the meeting successful from their perspective	As I noted, I have a number of questions for you to see about the possibilities for speeding up the software development engine and spend the rest of the time talking about what kinds of improvements might be possible here at ABC Technology. Does anyone else have anything besides what I've mentioned thus far that you'd like to cover? If you left this meeting today and you got everything out of it that you hoped to get, what would we need to do to get there?
Transition	Does anyone have any thoughts, comments, or questions before we jump in? Very well. One last thought: while we'll be starting with the presentation (or demonstration) on [topic], folks like yourselves always get the most out of it, and it's always a more interesting meeting, if we make it a discussion versus a presentation. I'll stop for questions as we go along, but feel free to jump in whenever you'd like.

As you introduce yourself and your company, establish credibility. You don't need much time to establish a firm foundation for your credibility, and you shouldn't overdo your introduction. Do not, however, assume that people know about you, your background, your business successes, your prominent positions, or your impressive associations.

The two most common mistakes salespeople make when introducing themselves are overdoing it and underdoing it.

- *Example—overdoing it:* My name is Dr. Emmett Brown and I am the world's most recognized authority on Flux Capacitors. Over the years, I've worked with DeLorean, GMAC, Ford, the Department of Defense . . . (26 companies later), and dozens of others. I've written 44 articles and 4 books on the topic. The first book is . . . the second one is . . . the third one is . . . I'm also a prominent speaker, including keynotes at . . . (10 minutes pass).
- *Example—underdoing it:* My name is Emmett and I've been working in the capacitor industry since 1985.
- *Example—just right:* For those of you that don't know me, I'm Dr. Emmett Brown, and I've been fascinated with flux capacitors for 20 years now. Along the way I've published a few dozen articles on the topic and I just finished my fourth book. My path in the industry has led me to work with some great companies such as DeLorean and Ford, most recently as the senior vice president of the capacitor division. Now that I've been consulting for five years, it's given me more flexibility to do some interesting things, like chair the Capacitor Association of North America Conference, teach in the engineering division at Cornell, and coach my son's Little League baseball team. (Elapsed time: 30 seconds.)

The idea is to communicate major, important points without seeming too self-absorbed. The more impressive your background and achievements, the more likely people will be to ask you about them later, or look you up themselves. You will be more intriguing if you give only a few major points and then move on.

Deliver on Your Promise During the First Call

We regularly prospect on the telephone to generate leads for our own services. Sometimes we use a best practice approach to set first meetings. A few months back, we had a meeting set up with

(continued)

the head of marketing of a company to discuss best practices in prospecting (ironic, yes?). As we got on the phone for the meeting, we were introduced to the CEO of the prospect company who was both a welcome and surprising addition to the meeting.

It did not start warmly. We checked with the CEO what he hoped to get out of the meeting. His response, "You said you would take 20 minutes and tell us a few things we don't know. So start talking." Although we couldn't see him, we knew he was sitting back in his chair, arms crossed, with a deep, furrowed brow.

We began our presentation about best practices, occasionally pausing to ask if there were questions. All we received as a response was, "Keep going."

About 15 minutes into the "conversation" we noted to the CEO that we were nearing the end of our allotted 20 minutes. Did he have anything we had discussed that he wanted to know more about? Did we miss anything he'd like to talk about?

"Yes. I have been getting these darn sales pitches from people like you for the last six months. You are the first to deliver what you said you would. I got more time. Let's talk about. . . ." If we were in his office, we are sure we would have seen him lean closer to the phone, unfurrow his brow, and maybe even smile.

The bait and switch is still en vogue with some people's sales pitches. Buyers are on to it. Make sure you deliver on the stated premise for your meeting.

Stage 3. Needs Discovery—Interest, Desire, Aspirations, and Afflictions

Structure this section of the meeting depending on the premise of the meeting. For example, if the premise is a presentation or product demo (e.g., best practices, how you've solved problems, research findings, product demonstration), then use this time to cover topics like:

- Company overview
- Background on the problem
- Typical solutions and their shortcomings

- Reasons why success or failure happens
- New research on the subject
- New approach/better approach/product demonstration
- Typical impact of failure and success
- Recommendations and actions to take
- Questions and discussion

It may seem counterintuitive that you can uncover needs by presenting, but it happens all the time. You stimulate thinking. For example, prospects often interject as you're presenting common challenges, "Well, we have number one and number four all set, but if we could only figure out a way to do something about number two and number three we'd be in much better shape. After two years of trying to tackle them, we're still at square one."

If your meeting was set on any of the following premises, it's usually best to skip presentations and jump right into aspiration and affliction discovery:

- They have expressed a felt need and want to discuss how you can help.
- You have been brought in by a third party who is trusted by the prospect and believes you can help.
- The meeting purpose is to establish a relationship for possible referral business.

If so, it is often still appropriate to give a presentation or demonstration after needs discovery, or, depending on the flow of the conversation, after your impact analysis. You might say something like, "Based on the discussion thus far, I'm fairly confident we can help. What I think would give you the best idea is if I took 15 minutes to share with you a few things about us so you can get a sense of where we might fit."

Engagement Point

At some point in a rainmaking conversation, a prospect either says to himself, "I'm not interested. Time to end this meeting." Or, "I'm intrigued. Time to engage more deeply and see where this goes."

(continued)

Your goal is, of course, to get as many of the latter as possible. Although Jerry Maguire might get them at hello, your engagement point can happen during introductions, during your needs discovery, during your presentation, or as you banter ideas and stories back and forth later in the discussion.

Whenever it happens, there's usually a specific time in the conversation that the prospect goes from passive engagement—they're "present" but not yet sure of either solving this challenge or if you will stay on their to-do lists—to active engagement, where they commit to themselves to move something forward.

We call this *the engagement point*—the time at which an outcome that would favor you goes on the prospect's to-do list.

As you move into your aspiration and affliction questioning, make sure you:

- State the big picture parameters of the discussion. You can say something like, "In these situations, there are five areas that need to come together to make success happen. A, B, C, D, and E."

  By putting bookends on the discussion and touching on major points, you set the direction of the rest of the conversation while you also build more credibility with your understanding of the situation as a whole.

- Ask questions in the various areas where the customer may have needs. If you've planned well for the discussion, you can further demonstrate your knowledge of the big picture by being thorough with your questions and comments.

- Summarize the key points of the discussion, so you're all on the same page before you move forward.

Stage 4. Impact Analysis

Your goal is to gather information on the key factors you need to know so you can figure out if you can help them, and with what impact.

Impact analysis typically happens in three stages:

1. Directly when you talk about aspirations and afflictions.
2. In a discussion specifically about impact.
3. In between meetings with the prospect.

In the first instance, you'll weave back and forth between aspirations and afflictions, and impact, throughout the discussion. For example, you might say, "So you're not getting the response you want from your e-mail marketing campaigns, and that's a problem for you. The response right now is about 8 percent in terms of open rate, and 0.8 percent on orders. Do you have a sense of what the difference is to you if you could increase the open rate by a percent or two, or the order rate by a tenth of a percent?"

Once you know what you need to know, you work to make sure *the prospect* understands the impact.

A powerful way to do this is to stand up at the whiteboard (if there is one) or draw on a piece of paper and begin to outline the factors you've already uncovered. This could look like your impact model chart on page 78. You write the impact model factor, ask the question to get to the impact, and write it down.

If the impact is hidden and you're helping the buyer piece it all together, this part of the conversation can take a while. It might be as simple as getting the buyer to state, "Well, if we were to decrease turnover by 5 percent and increase our hiring efficiency by 10 percent, that would easily be worth $2 million." Or, "Yes, if we could get our orders from our e-mail effort up by 0.1 percent, that's $30,000 per month in increased sales."

The third point at which impact analysis happens is after the meeting. Often you can't get a sense of what the impact will be without further analysis. Perhaps you need to involve a technical professional to see what's possible or to get to a finer point on the details.

If this is the case, you can close this portion of the meeting by interesting the prospect in what you'll share with her when you've done your impact analysis.

For example, you could say:

"Just to summarize, you have A, B, and C going on. When we've seen this at other companies, we know that on the surface it doesn't seem like a big issue, but, after taking a hard look, company leaders see these issues are costing your company between $50,000 and $150,000 per month in lost profit margin. At your size, this is significant.

"Before I have the sense of what's really possible here, I have to work with my team (or I need to do more analysis) to see how, given what we've learned today, we'd approach building a solution. That will drive the particulars of whether or not we'd be able to achieve the same type of savings, and what the various options are to get there."

Stage 5. New Reality

Like impact, you should be sowing the seeds of the possible new reality for the customer throughout your conversations

As you work with customers to bring to light the impact of solving aspirations and afflictions, they'll start to envision for themselves and feel what it's like to have the solutions in place.

> **Influence Tip: Getting the Buyer to State Impact and New Reality**
>
> President Dwight Eisenhower described leadership as the art of getting someone to do something because they want to do it. Sales works that way, too: The more a prospect wants to take action, the more likely he will.
>
> One way to do that is to have *the prospect* state impact, and have *the prospect* describe the new reality, using the influence principle of involvement.
>
> Here's how it might look:

You: "So we have two major problems on the table then, yes?"

Prospect: "Indeed. Development time and scheduling."

You: "I'm curious to hear what you think might happen if you were to tackle the problems."

Prospect: "Well, I can see that we could speed up our software development time by 20 percent. Maybe more. But let's say 20 percent for now."

You: "What effect do you think that would have on your team?"

Prospect: "Well, I mentioned we're struggling to launch three new software products per year. This will get us to four, maybe five. The team will feel much more accomplished as well, and that will help morale and quality."

> You: "What's a new software title worth in revenue to you on average?"
>
> Prospect: "Well, we have about a 65 percent market success rate, so altogether somewhere between $2 million and $3 million in revenue."
>
> You: "Except for marketing support and distribution, are there additional costs when you launch a new title?"
>
> Prospect: "Not much. Now that I think about it, we'll push average margin higher as well. If we have the same team developing more titles, then I can see us with a 60 percent margin or higher on each title."

Similar to highlighting the impact, you can summarize the new reality during the meeting on the whiteboard in front of the room, or on your computer screen if you're meeting on the web. Writing the basic "before" and "after" is as powerful in the moment as it will be in your follow-up documents and proposal.

Stage 6. Determine FAINT and Buying Process

Many a salesperson wraps up with how great the discussion was, sets next steps, and closes the meeting without clarifying or determining the buying process.

You have just spent quite some time uncovering and confirming need, but at some point you need to continue to determine anything yet to be uncovered in FAINT (financial capacity, authority, interest, need, and timing) and the buying process:

- Confirm continued *interest.*
- Determine buying *authority,* buying process, and *time frame.*
- Involve appropriate decision makers.
- Determine *financial capacity* or *funds* to move forward.

Confirm continued interest: Asking people if they're interested in moving forward can build excitement and create commitment on the part of prospects. If you ask, "From my perspective, it seems like there's a fairly compelling case to be made for continuing to move the discussion forward. Are you interested in doing so?"

If you get a yes, you can further clarify by asking, "Great. Since we discussed a great deal today, I'm curious to know if anything in particular is rising above the rest to make you say that." Their answers can give you insight on what's most important to them. Prompt them if they miss anything big.

Answers like this also plant the seeds in people's minds that they want to move forward. Thinking something is one thing, but saying it out loud, especially in front of other people, will increase your chances of getting positive outcomes.

If you get a no, or if some people in the room say yes and others say no or are noncommittal, you have the potential to turn it around. If you have detractors and you allow them to talk with other decision makers while you are not in the room, it's likely they'll kill your sale.

Determine buying authority, buying process, and time frame: There's a possibility that you're speaking to the person who can make a decision, but you don't want to leave that to chance.

The tricky part here is asking about the power players without insulting someone who isn't. It's tempting to ask, "Are you the decision maker?" and "Who are the other decision makers?" but you should ask more subtly, "If we were to move forward, what would be the process on your end? Who are the other people that need to be involved and what are their roles?"

If he says something like, "I'm the key decision maker and will find and approve funds to move forward if it makes sense for our strategy," then it's likely you have found the nexus of buying power. If he stops short of saying this, then you can ask him, "If we were to move forward, who are the people that would need to actually sign off and give any final yeses before you could put something in motion?"

If he's not the buying authority and he says things like, "Well, it would go up to our COO eventually, and I'd need to pitch to them why we want to move forward," then, in most situations, you'll need to gain access to the COO.

If the prospect hasn't already mentioned time frame, it's best to ask about it simply. "Assuming you decide this is worthwhile to do, can you give me a sense of when you'd like to get underway?"

Involve appropriate decision makers: Less successful salespeople tend to do everything in the sales process for the buyer. They think, "If I make it easy to buy—if the buyer has to do practically nothing in the process except answer questions and sign the contract—then I'll have the greatest chance at winning."

The flaw in this thinking concerns what drives buyer ownership and commitment. There's nothing wrong with making the buying process as straightforward as possible, but getting emotional investment in the process is a powerful influence strategy. To get emotional investment, you can:

- Have a brainstorming session with the decision makers as a step before you craft the solution.
- Ask the prospect to gather certain pieces of information for you that will help you craft the best solution.
- Interview a series of influencers to the sale so you can better understand how to craft a solution that will work best for them.
- Ask the prospect to join you at your office for a meeting instead of your going to his.

Each of these activities takes time and thinking on behalf of the prospect. Any time prospects spend both time thinking, and energy on something, they're making an investment.

The more invested they are, the more they will want to see something come out of it.

Determine financial capacity or funds: You need to determine if prospects have the financial ability to move forward. Let's say you're working directly with the CEO of a $10 billion company for a $500,000 purchase. In this scenario, you don't even need to determine financial ability. If the CEO wants to do something, that person has the ability to spend $500,000. In a company of this size, it's close to a rounding error.

In most situations, however, you want to give prospects the overall sense of how much something is likely to cost after they admit the aspirations and afflictions, see the impact of doing something about them, and have a sense of the new reality. This may take one meeting and it may take several, but you want to bring up the ballpark range—and it can be a big ballpark—once you and the buyer have a sense of these factors.

You: "You've just mentioned that speeding up the software engineering process here is probably worth $2 million to $3 million in increased margin per year. Over the course of three years that's $6 million to $9 million in margin. Given what we've discussed, and how our process works, it's probably going to take between $250,000 and $400,000 to make these kinds of improvements.

"We're not there yet, but if we get to the point where you're confident that we can actually achieve the improvements, would you be willing and able to move forward?"

By asking it like this, you're positioning it as an investment and return, not as a budgetary concern. You're not asking the prospect to commit to buying, and you're not asking him, "How does it sound?" because the answer will most often be, "It sounds high."

Later in the process—not in the early calls—when you have your solution crafted you will be ready to respond to objections and negotiate if needed. At first, you want to norm the buyer to the idea of spending what he needs to spend.

It will also be the case here and there that he says, "We'd never spend that much" or "We don't have that kind of money." This is necessary to know as well, because you can then move on to other prospecting and selling efforts.

Stage 7. Next Steps

Assuming everything is in order at this point, it's time to close the discussion and set next steps. Now you should:

- Confirm reasons to continue.
- Suggest and calibrate next steps.
- Gain agreement on next meeting time and purpose.

You say something like, "Jennifer, it was great speaking with you today. It seems like there's a strong fit, and that there are a number of ways we can work together."

"In terms of next steps, I'll go back to my office and write up a summary of today's discussion and send it to you. Over the next week, I'll meet with my technical team and subject-matter experts and prepare three options for moving forward for you to react to."

"We'll then meet at our office to go through them. You'll be there, as well as bringing your VP and EVP of engineering to introduce them to this process. We'll probably need a morning to go through everything. Does that work for you?"

(Assuming it does) "Okay, then, how about Thursday the 14th at 8:30 AM."

If the process doesn't work, then continue the discussion to find out what does work.

What you want is a firm next step (e.g., a meeting on the 14th at 8:30 AM) and what you want to avoid is a fuzzy, open-ended next step. Open-ended next steps are when the prospect says, "Yes, put together those solutions and e-mail them to me. Then I'll get back to you with what we think we should do."

If you accept, you won't have her involvement or ownership. You'll change the dynamic of peer to subservience, and you'll weaken your chance at winning.

At all costs, you should maintain your peer relationship, and regularly negotiate next steps to keep her involved and moving the process forward. If you're willing to invest a lot of time and energy, and the buyer isn't willing to invest at least some, she's not invested enough in the process.

Stage 8. Meeting Follow Up

Depending on the next steps, you might have some information to gather and send, a discussion letter to write, or a proposal to prepare.

However you follow up, make sure you do it thoughtfully and completely.

Salespeople who only follow up with brief e-mails that say, "It was great meeting with you to discuss how we can help you address these major challenges. Our next step is to . . ." don't stand out from the crowd, and don't add value to the discussion.

One way to stand out and to continue to influence the process is to write a discussion letter.

Discussion letters should flow from the conversation, summarize and strengthen your position, and confirm next steps. Good discussion letters[1] have the following elements:

---

[1] For an example of a discussion letter, see the Appendix and Online Resources.

- Situation summary
- Aspirations and afflictions
- Impact
- New reality possibilities (if early in the process) or solution (if close to proposal)
- Credibility enhancement
- Buying process facilitation
- Next step

When it's time to propose, don't try to sell with your proposal. A proposal should be confirmation of how to move forward, not a persuasive document meant to sell for you. If you haven't yet presented a solution and the potential buyers ask for a proposal, it's usually too early. They are probably not at the stage where they're committed enough to move forward. A discussion letter can be a great bridge to building continued belief in your process, trust in you, ownership of the process, and desire to move forward.

Plus, if the buyer agrees with your discussion letter, in many cases, all you need to do to make it a proposal is to provide a place to sign.

PART THREE

MAXIMIZING YOUR RAIN SELLING SUCCESS

13

Prospecting by Phone

Creating Rainmaking Conversations

I've always found the harder I worked, the better my luck was.

—Ed Bradley

Prospecting—the act of creating new conversations that lead to sales—is perhaps the most overanalyzed of all the stages in the sales process. It's also one of the most misunderstood. The dynamics of how prospecting works continue to baffle many.

Prospecting is misunderstood. Then, when people seek to understand it better, they find conflicting advice. Different situations rightly call for different approaches, so some of the experts themselves are confused about what works and what doesn't. Some experts even tout their own approaches such as no-more-cold-calling lead generation methods for the purposes of selling their wares by preying on the emotional baggage that many people have about picking up the phone.

For those of you who want to succeed with prospecting and join the ranks of true rainmakers, it's important for you to see, without the smoke and mirrors, how selling with the telephone actually works. Then you can make your own decisions about what will work best for you.

We focus on the telephone because it's the most common way (with notable exceptions) that rainmakers use to create rainmaking conversations, even now in the second decade of the twenty-first century.

Prospecting—What It Is

There's an age-old formula in direct marketing referred to as AIDA. AIDA stands for Attention, Interest, Desire, and Action.

The goal of prospecting is to capture attention and create interest and then convert that interest into a conversation.

Note that we didn't say the goal of prospecting is to find someone currently looking to purchase a particular product or service. For most, this is *not* what you want to do, because it doesn't work often enough.

Goal of prospecting: To capture and create interest and then convert that interest into a conversation.

When prospecting you will find people who are already in the *Desire Phase* (someone interested in solving a particular problem or purchasing a known type of product or service) or the *Action Phase* (someone already in the process of searching for a solution to the problem), but if your approach is only to look for these people, you're in for a number of rude awakenings:

- Find someone who is already looking to buy, and they likely have a front-runner in mind. This front-runner is not you.
- If you don't sell a commodity product or service, it's likely that the buyer isn't considering buying what you offer because she doesn't know much (if anything) about it, how it works, and why it's worthwhile.
- Find someone who has the desire to solve a problem and hasn't yet started looking into how to do it, and you're in luck! But finding these people will be rare.

If you are the one who can capture *Attention* and stimulate *Interest* and *Desire*, you will be the front-runner, you will shape the prospect's understanding of the importance of solving a particular problem, and you will be in pole position to persuade them into *Action*.

> **Latent need:** The buyer has a need to solve something, but it's hidden beneath the surface. The buyer does not yet perceive the need, or doesn't perceive it strongly or clearly enough to act. Your job is to bring the need to the surface, define the need, and define and communicate the impact on the buyer's business.
>
> **Explicit need:** The buyer perceives a need to solve a problem. Your job is to explore the need, other possible needs, the issues creating and surrounding those needs, and define and communicate the impact on the buyer's business of working with you.

Before we get to prospecting tactics, it's important for you to consider the following question: Who drives the demand—you (the seller) or the prospect (the buyer)?

Demand Driven—The Buyer Drives the Demand to Buy

With a *demand-driven* offering, regardless of what you do for prospecting, you have to wait for the need to arise before you have an opportunity to sell something.

Suppose you are a litigation attorney. You can sell your heart out, but until someone gets sued or decides to sue, they're not hiring you or anyone else. No matter how good a salesperson a roofer might be, it's unlikely you will hire them to reroof your house if the roof is not 30 years old or leaking.

It's not hard to understand the concept. Demand driven: Until it is actually needed, it is not needed (or wanted, or purchased).

In this case, you're selling to *explicit need*. With explicit need, the buyer perceives a need to solve a problem. Your first job is to explore the need, other possible needs, the issues creating and surrounding those needs, and then define and communicate the impact on the business of working with you.

Demand Driving—The Seller Drives the Demand to Buy

With a *demand-driving* product or service, you can create opportunities and influence someone to purchase from you whether or not you or your offerings are currently on their radar. In fact, they may not even be aware that what you can provide even exists.

In this case, you'll typically be selling to *latent* need. With latent need, the buyer has a need to solve something, but it's hidden beneath the surface. He does not yet perceive the need, or doesn't perceive it strongly enough or clearly enough to act. Your first job is to bring the need to the surface, clarify what it is, and define and communicate the impact on the business.

Example of *Demand-Driving* Offerings

There are technology companies that sell software and systems that monitor the performance and uptime of computer systems, servers, and other technologies. Until there was a technology to monitor these, they were monitored by people. If buyers didn't know that technologies existed to do the monitoring for them, they wouldn't go looking for them.

It's up to the technology company—often solely the salespeople—to drive the demand for products.

The concept of demand-driving products and services is a little more complicated than demand driven, but not much. Demand-driving product or service: It is needed, it is wanted, and it could provide substantial value in the right situation, but the prospective customer may not perceive the need or the existence of the solution. You have to bring it up for them to see it.

Prospecting for Demand-Driven Services

When you are prospecting for a *demand-driven* product or service, you need to be either remembered or easily found at the elusive time a buyer perceives a need. Thus, your prospecting efforts will focus on getting on the radar screens of the potential clients and *remaining there* until the elusive time of need arises. As you stay on the radar screen, your job is to create a preference to work with you should the need arise for your products and services.

If the prospect is currently buying from someone else, you need to supplant the other provider by creating a sense of dissatisfaction with what they're getting from the other provider, or by creating a sense of dissatisfaction with their overall situation.

Prospecting with Demand-Driving Offerings

When you are selling a *demand-driving* offering you need to focus on generating interest in solving a particular affliction (problem) or achieving some kind of aspiration (goal).

You need to capture attention first because prospects won't buy if they don't know that you or your solution exist. Then you need to generate interest by piquing curiosity and interest in addressing the issues. Next, you need to create desire to move forward, desire to move forward with you and your solution, and help the prospect purchase from you.

Your prospecting is likely to look much different, however, from firms that serve demand-driven buyers. Instead of a mission to stay on the radar screen and wait for a need to arise, you'll be on a mission to inspire, educate, and influence.

A Closer Look at Cold Calls

In our *How Clients Buy* benchmark research study, we asked buyers two related questions about cold calls:

1. Do you ever accept cold calls?
2. What factors are important to you in accepting the call?

Four in 10 buyers (42 percent) indicated that they accept cold calls. The two *most* important factors for them in accepting a cold call are:

1. I see a need for the offering, now or in the future.
2. The provider offers me something of value on the call—best practices, research findings, discussions with experts and practitioners, event invitations.

Both of these factors were considered at least "very important" by more than 80 percent of buyers who accept cold calls. The least important factor in accepting a cold call, though still considered "very important" by a majority, was dissatisfaction with the current provider, as shown in Figure 13.1.

Each factor we tested ranged from approximately 52 percent to 93 percent "extremely" or "very" important to buyers regarding whether they

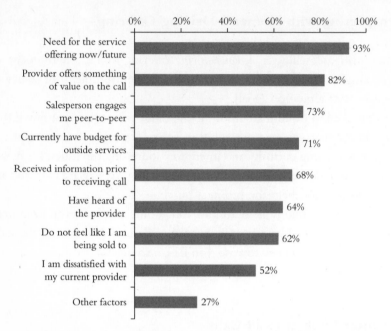

**Figure 13.1   Importance of Factors in Whether Buyers
Accept Cold Calls**

take a cold call. With many of these factors, it's within your power to stack the deck in your favor when selling by telephone. Let's take a closer look.

Need (93 percent): If you target your buyers well, you are most likely to find buyers with a need to use the products and services you offer. Target poorly or have a subpar database and the odds move significantly against you.

Meanwhile, remember: Many of the buyers *may not know they have a need* because you haven't driven the demand yet. The need is latent. They'll see the need after you open their eyes to it.

Value delivered on the call (82 percent): Once someone answers the phone, you have seconds to keep them from hanging up. If they perceive that continuing is a waste of time . . . end of call. You're in complete control of what you say when someone answers the phone, so it's up to you to come up with a message that buyers in your market will find valuable. The exact message will differ for each firm and each buyer. The only constant is that rarely does "buy from me" or "listen to my capabilities pitch" work as the primary reason for a prospect to agree to a meeting.

Peer-to-peer (73 percent) and *Don't feel like I'm being sold to (62 percent):* Before you make the calls, ask yourself: "Am I ready to be perceived as a peer with the top people I'm calling?" If you feel like you are intruding or are nervous about picking up the phone and talking to that senior executive, you won't come across as a peer. Do you have the skills and confidence to do so? If not, start practicing.

Received information prior to the call (68 percent): Cold calling works, but it works even better if you have paved the way with valuable information ahead of time. It helps if you send something worthwhile and intriguing beforehand is not necessary, but it helps.

Have heard of provider (64 percent): It's within your power to build your brand. Even if you can't affect the brand perception of the entire company for the entire marketplace, you can work on a set of buyers with your own efforts. If you do, you'll be a brand reputation–building machine of one.

FAINT—The New Definition of a Qualified Prospect

A typical definition of a qualified prospect used by many sales managers is BANT. A buyer is qualified if they have:

- **B**udget
- **A**uthority
- **N**eed
- **T**ime frame to buy

BANT works when a buyer:

- Knows they're going to buy something.
- Knows what they've paid for it in the past, or knows "what it goes for."
- Can define for themselves what needs to happen to produce the outcome they want.

But many purchases in business don't happen like this. Unplanned purchases, including most demand-driving products and services, won't have a budget allocated.

This is why it's important to retire BANT as a definition. Salespeople who only follow BANT end up, by definition, disqualifying

(continued)

buyers who don't have a budget. Even when prospects don't have one, if other conditions are met, the prospects are often still qualified.

Imagine for a minute that you are a company that helps billion-dollar institutions, like hospital systems, reduce their overhead spending. The CFO of a hospital might be happy to reduce spending, but most likely his attention is focused on other things, like financing a new wing and hiring the best doctors and nurses. His first concern is not his spending on rubber gloves and janitorial services.

One client of RAIN Group helps hospital systems reduce their overhead spending by 10 percent or more. A billion-dollar hospital system might spend $110 million on overhead, so that's $11 million in savings a year. They can certainly drive demand for such a service. Spend one dollar to save 10 dollars . . . our client sells this product to hospitals all the time.

Imagine, however, if our client had asked the CFO, "What's your budget for this product?" Silly question: He doesn't have one. What he does have is the authority to spend, and if our client can communicate the value of their offering clearly (a 10 to 1 return), the CFO certainly has the ability to make a decision to buy, even if he doesn't have a budget.

Unplanned purchases, including almost all demand-driving products and services, won't have a budget allocated.

FAINT—the new definition of a qualified buyer—stands for:

Financial Capacity: Focus initially on organizations and buyers who have the financial capacity or funds to buy from you. They may not have a budget, but they have the overall financial wherewithal to spend. Sell where the money is.

Authority: Focus on finding individuals who have the authority to make decisions on how to use funds. You must deal with the people who have the authority to allocate said funds.

Interest: Generate interest in learning what's possible and how the buyer might achieve a new and better reality than the one they have today.

Need: Uncover specific needs you can solve. They're likely to be latent—hidden beneath the surface—but they're there if you can uncover them, much like the hospital example noted previously.

Timing: Establish purchase intent and a specific time frame for buying. This might take a number of conversations, might involve a number of decision makers and influencers, and might take some time to do. Once you do it, however, you now have a qualified prospect and a real opportunity in your pipeline.

If you're selling a value-added product or service, one that presents a compelling business case to a buyer to engage, think FAINT, not BANT.

Key Concepts in Prospecting

Before you begin your prospecting efforts, keep in mind the following Key Concepts.

Targeting

The foundation that underpins prospecting success is the strength of your list and the precision of your targeting. Salespeople often call too low in the organization and try to start a groundswell by working their way up. Call high to decision makers. Make sure that your list is clean and ready to go before you start, or you'll find your day is lost in fits and starts.[1]

Value in Every Touch

When you sell, no one wants to hear your capabilities pitch, your history, or your life story right off the bat. They're looking to find out how their lives can be enriched by working with you.

    When you think about providing value, don't just think about the value you will provide after they buy from you. Think about the value they'll get just from speaking with you. Eventually you'll sell your company, your offering, and yourself. At first, sell the idea that the prospects' time will be well spent if they elect to speak with you.

---

[1] See the Appendix and Online Resources for a list of 10 list-building resources.

The Right Offer

Your ultimate offer might be a particular type of software, technical instrument, building materials, financial product, operations plan, or marketing tactic. But the interim offers—the offers you make and they accept *before* they buy from you—must be crafted with the utmost care.

No Tricks

Plenty of business success awaits you with your high-integrity approach. There is no need to use tricks, bend the truth, or cut corners to generate your initial conversations. Anything that you wouldn't feel comfortable telling your children about when you tuck them in bed at night, leave out of your selling techniques.

Multiple Touches

It takes more attempts than most people think to get through to your top prospects. It can often take seven or more touches to get through to someone. That number goes up and down—across different industries and when you reach out to different titles. What's always true: It takes more attempts to get through to your targets than many people think.

Variety of Touches

Cold calling works well alone, but it works even better with mail (yes, we are talking snail mail here) and e-mail touches.

Six Essential Prospecting Outreach Formulas

There are essentially six different formulas that work for telephone calls, e-mail, and sales letters. Although all are part of the way to create conversation with prospects, we look at them in the context of telephone calls. You can, however, apply the same formulas to e-mail and letters.

The six approaches are:

1. *Best practice approach:* You deliver value by offering the prospect a chance to learn how others have solved a particular problem or achieved an aspiration.
2. *Straight results approach:* You share results, and engender interest from the buyer to find out how you did it.
3. *New idea approach:* You deliver value by bringing your ideas directly to the table.
4. *New and different approach:* You deliver value in the call by educating the prospect on a new, innovative, or uncommon way to solve a problem or achieve an aspiration.
5. *First step approach:* You deliver value by offering the prospect something worthwhile and easy to accept as a nonthreatening introduction to you.
6. *Can you help me approach:* You deliver value by appealing to the desire to help someone else deliver value and succeed.

Along with the first six, in some instances you can consider the *capabilities or demonstration approach* in which you deliver value by communicating what you can do.

We pin the tail on this donkey for the most part, but in some situations, such as when, for whatever reason, your demonstration offer is amazing, you can use the approach. Meanwhile, it's usually best to use one of the other approaches, and then weave your demonstration or capabilities in as the conversation warrants.

What's In It For Me (WIIFM)—The Common Denominator in All Outreach Formulae

Let's assume you're a chief strategy officer at an $800 million manufacturing firm in Ohio. Someone calls you unexpectedly and says, "My name is John Smith and I'm a strategy and change management consultant. Do you need help building strategy or managing change? Let's meet." Even if you have an empty calendar for the next three weeks, your immediate change needs probably won't include John Smith.

Let's give John a second chance. He calls the same person and this time says, "My name is John Smith with Arc Strategy. We've never spoken before. The reason I'm calling is my firm has recently conducted a major benchmark study on how manufacturing businesses—including your two major competitors—in the Midwest are successfully working with their labor unions in the face of global outsourcing. While there are three practices that are working in general, a few practices fail almost every place we studied. (PAUSE) As a way of introducing ourselves, I'd be happy to come by and take you through what we've found. The results are eye opening, to say the least."

If this topic is on his mind, he might risk a half hour to hear the results. Or he might have some questions right then and there. Either way, if I'm John, I've presented a cold introduction of myself and my firm to his company in a way that delivers value.

Will everyone take John up on this meeting? Of course not. If, however, the target list is well built, a good number of prospects will.

Whichever approach you choose, the prospect has to see value *in the meeting itself*. Eventually the prospect may get value out of your products and services, but for now, you need to sell the value of a first conversation.

Here are examples of six value-based call approaches.

BEST PRACTICE APPROACH

Call component	What you say
Name	Sharon, this is Lee Adama.
Organization	I'm with Caprica City Technologies.
Introduction—direct	We've never spoken before,
What we do	But we focus on working with pharmaceutical companies to help run the most efficient clinical trials . . .
Aspiration or affliction, couched in *best practice* (Capture attention)	The reason I'm calling is we've just completed a major benchmark research study to identify the key drivers of cost reduction and speed improvement in clinical trials, and at the same time, maintain high quality standards . . . PAUSE

Call component	What you say
Offer (Generate interest)	I'll be in southern New Jersey on June 14 and 15 at a client site. As a way of introducing ourselves, I'd be happy to come by and take a few minutes to share with you the research results. I think you'll find them pretty eye opening.
Call to action	I was looking at the 14th in the afternoon or the 15th in the morning to meet?

STRAIGHT RESULTS APPROACH

Call component	What you say
Name	Bill, I'm Helena Cain.
Organization	I'm with Pegasus Fundraising.
Introduction—trigger	I read in the *Chronicle of Higher Education* that you just joined Gemanon College as their new vice president of development.
What we do	We focus on working with college and university development organizations . . .
Aspiration or affliction, couched in *results achieved* (Capture attention)	. . . to help them increase their fundraising results by an average of 15 percent per campaign. We recently completed successful campaigns with state university and the College of Astral Queen . . . PAUSE
Offer (Generate interest)	I saw in your alumni magazine that your fundraising goal for this coming year is about $40 million . . . a 15 percent increase would be $6 million more.
Call to action	Are you available next Tuesday or Wednesday in the morning to see how we might get those results for you?

NEW IDEA APPROACH

Call component	What you say
Name	Saul, my name is Aaron Doral.
Organization	I'm with Basestar Innovation.
Introduction—direct	We've never spoken before,
What we do	But we focus on working with consumer packaged goods companies to help them innovate . . .
Aspiration or affliction the prospect *has stated* (Capture attention)	The reason I'm calling is I was just on your web site and saw a note in a press release that you were looking for any and all ideas on how you can leverage open innovation . . .
Offer (Generate interest)	Open innovation is what we do, and, given your strategy to lead in dental products, we have three ideas that we think you might find intriguing . . . PAUSE. Perhaps these three ideas could spark some interesting conversation.
Call to action	Are you available to discuss these ideas next Tuesday morning or Wednesday morning?

NEW AND DIFFERENT METHOD APPROACH

Call component	What you say
Name	Karl, I'm Laura Roslin.
Organization	I'm with Picon Strategies.
Introduction—referral	Your COO Jim Smith suggested that I give you a call.
What we do	We work with technology companies to help them get their salespeople up to speed as experts in their fields and selling full tilt very quickly after they are hired.

Call component	What you say
Aspiration or affliction, couched in *results achieved* (Capture attention)	The reason I'm calling is that we've been working with companies such as Centurion and Viper Systems to help them reduce their ramp-up times for new sales reps by 50 percent, while at the same time decreasing new rep turnover by 15 percent in a breakthrough new way . . . PAUSE
Offer (Generate interest)	How we've solved the problem is pretty different than, I'm guessing, anything you've seen. But we won't know that until we share it with you.
Call to action	Right now I am looking to discuss our approach next Tuesday morning or Wednesday morning—which works best for you?

FIRST STEP APPROACH

Call component	What you say
Name	Kara, this is Felix Gaeta.
Organization	I'm with C-Bucks Financial.
Introduction—referral	Sam Anders in your Springfield office suggested I give you a call.
What we do	For the past 12 years we've focused on helping owners of family businesses in the $10 million to $50 million range transfer ownership of their firms and realize a liquidity event when they want one . . .
Aspiration or affliction, couched in *easy to accept offer* (Capture attention)	The reason I'm calling is we are having a private, CEO-only dinner and speaker event at the Copley Plaza in downtown Boston where CEOs will have a chance to talk with each other and enjoy our speaker, the dean of Triton University Business School . . . PAUSE

(*continued*)

FIRST STEP APPROACH (*continued*)

Call component	What you say
Offer (Generate interest)	As we've never met, I'd look forward to doing so by having you come to the event as my guest.
Call to action	Can I put you down as a yes for the event?

CAN YOU HELP ME APPROACH

Call component	What you say
Name	Callie, this is Tory Foster.
Organization	I'm with Colonial One.
Introduction	We've never spoken before,
What we do	But we focus on helping HR leaders hire the best candidates for leadership positions using our proprietary assessment instruments.
Aspiration or affliction, couched in *results achieved* (Capture attention)	We have been able to increase new hire retention and success rates at companies in the banking industry by 25 percent. PAUSE.
Offer (Generate interest)	I'm calling to see if you might be interested in engaging a discussion about how we achieve these results, but I don't know who at your company [NAME] would be the right person to talk to.
Call to action	Can you point me in the right direction?

PAUSE

Pauses are great in telephone calling because people like to fill silence. When you pause after an intriguing statement, it gives the prospect a chance to ask you a question. Once they do that, you know you have captured their attention and you're on the path to building interest.

If they jump in on a pause and say, "I'm not interested," you can turn the call around with the strategies that follow. If you haven't yet gotten to your offer, you can say, "Before I let you go, though, can I ask you one question?" Once you get the okay (you'll find you'll often get one) proceed with the rest of your initial call strategy and your offer.

Telephone Call Success Power Boosters

Inserting the call success power boosters listed below will enhance your success. We have them inserted throughout our earlier six examples to show you what they might look like. Below is an explanation of each:

- *Trigger event.* Changes in circumstances create need. A trigger event is an occurrence that might create (or trigger) the impetus for the prospect organization to do or change something. The trigger event could be a merger, a key new hire, a new competitive threat, a milestone achieved, or a new strategy launched. Always be on the lookout for trigger events and reference them in your calls. You can use technologies like Google alerts to give you up-to-the-moment news on your prospects.
- *Research.* If you have done your homework about your target company before you call, you show that you are serious about how you can help them and that you are not just spraying and praying with random dialing. Demonstrate interest in them and you demonstrate your customer-focused approach and willingness to work hard.
- *Referral.* If you call someone based on a referral, you carry the referrer on the call with you (a most powerful companion). For example, if you say, "Jim Smith, your COO, suggested I give you a call," the person is more likely to hear you out because they wouldn't want Jim to think they hung up on someone he sent their way.
- *Social proof.* The company you keep shines like a halo over your head. If you are able to name drop that you've worked with a specific Fortune 500 company or a significant player in their industry or even a local, well-respected company, this will communicate to a prospect that you travel and work in the right circles. Just make sure you insert the name in a way that enhances your image and does not scream name dropper.
- *Experience.* Let people know how long you've been working in a particular industry and in what context. If you've been around

for a while, it helps up front to let people know that you're not the new guy (assuming you're not the new guy). Explicitly demonstrate your experience in working with their situation or industry, as in our example above, "For the last 12 years we've focused on helping *owners of family businesses.*"

Prospecting with Referrals

If a contact responds to you on the phone like this, "Sounds interesting, but the person you need to speak with is Jane Johnson . . . give her a call," don't just accept the referral and say good-bye. Ask them, "Would you be willing to make a quick co-introduction by e-mail so she knows why I'm calling?"

If the person says, "Sure," (and, of course, follows through), it's much more likely you'll be able to make the next connection to Jane. If they say, "Sure" and don't do it, you are no worse off and you can still call Jane. And if they say, "Nah, just give her a call," then you're still in the same boat. They'll never say, "I take it back now, don't use my name."

You have nothing to lose and everything to gain by asking.

Any one of the call approaches we have shared will work, but they certainly will not work 100 percent of the time. You will run into buyers that resist. You just interrupted them. Their minds were on something else. They don't know you. The initial attempt to capture their attention might not work, but don't retreat immediately from the first "No, thanks. Not interested." There are quite a number of ways to make a save. The important part is to not give up right away.

Here are some push backs you will most likely get from prospects in the process of calling, and how you can turn them around.

PUSH BACK 1: I'M NOT INTERESTED

Prospect: "I'm not interested."

You: "Okay. I'm curious to know, though. What could I have said about this that might have actually interested you?"

Prospect: "Nothing, really."

You: "Then if I hear correctly, it's not that the topic's not interesting to you, it's that you're not interested in talking at all right now. You're focused on something else."

Prospect: "You got it."

You: "Then let's not talk right now, but is it your area to focus on improving marketing returns at your company? Are you the person who that would fall under?"

Prospect: "Yes, I am."

You: "Well, when I speak with companies, even those that don't think there's the ability to increase their e-mail marketing efficiency by 10 percent at least, the opportunity is usually there. Whether it's there or not, I think you'll get some value out of the conversation because I'll share with you that best practice research about how it's been done at places like (big industry player name here). Can we talk at another time, maybe on Friday at 2 or 3? That way you can give me a few minutes to pique your interest, and if I don't, all you risk is the time in exchange for insight."

Prospect: "Okay, sure. Let's talk at 2 PM this Friday."

PUSH BACK 2: NOW'S NOT A GOOD TIME

Prospect: "Now's not a good time."

You: "Do you mean for talking about it, or is it that increasing your sales performance just isn't something that is a top priority right now?"

Prospect: "Neither."

You: "Why is that? Sometimes when that's the case it's because the company isn't looking to grow revenue for one reason or another. Is that it?"

Prospect: "Oh, we'd like to grow revenue, but it's just been so tough with the merger happening that all of our attention is focused there."

You: "You mean merging the two sales forces from Apollo and Kobol, yes? I saw that on your web site. It's one of the reasons I called. Has that been a challenge?"

Prospect: "Yes, we are, and we're having a heck of a time moving past 'merger mode' and into 'action mode.'"

(continued)

You: "I'm going to guess that one sales force is still selling their old area and same with the second, yes? And perhaps there are other issues distracting the sales forces and making them focus less on sales, and more on, well, internal gyrations.
Prospect: "That and more."
You: "We focus on sales-force integration with mergers. Again, that is the reason I called. It's common that two sales forces, when merged together, mix about as well as milk and Pepsi. At least at first. But we've been able to turn that around. Would you like to hear how?" (PAUSE)
Prospect: "Okay, well, it's still not a good time, but later in the week might work."

It can be a good sign when prospects say they're already working with a competitor because it means they have the need, they see the value, and they buy your category of product or service.

Your job is to start planting the seeds of why this prospect should buy from you. Here are three ways you can respond to the incumbent push back:

1. "Good to hear. I'm curious, what do you think makes the relationship work so well?" This is a relatively nonthreatening way to get key insight into the buyer's mind-set. It gets the prospect talking. And based on what he says, you can probe further and uncover areas where there may be issues with the current provider or holes in their offerings. After the prospect talks for a little bit, you can ask a series of "I'm curious to know" questions.

   For example, let's say you're selling network and data security technology to banks. You can say, "Great to hear. I'm curious to know, though, if they have 24-hour support if something goes haywire on you?" or "I'm curious to know if they talked with you about the last papers from the last industry conference and the trends that are sweeping through the industry?" or "I'm curious to know if their most recent release will allow you to access all of your intrusion detection data in real time?" If you get any "no" answers, that leaves you room to explore more.

   You might ask, "What topics do you cover in your monthly meetings with your current provider?" In most cases, the answer to that question is going to be, "We don't have monthly meetings." This gives you an opportunity to demonstrate how working with you is different. For example, you might say something like, "Would you like to know what we cover in the monthly meetings we have with clients?"

2. "It sounds like things are pretty good. But you didn't say they were doing an amazing job. What would it look like if a company was doing an amazing job by your standards?" By asking that question you get the prospect thinking about where the current provider may not be meeting expectations. It also gets them thinking about what it might be like if they did switch.

3. "Glad to hear that things are going well. While I am not too familiar with their process, I do know it's always worthwhile to have a second set of eyes to look things over. The next time you have something like this, I'd be happy to give it a quick review to see if we'd approach it any differently. If nothing else, you'll get a different perspective and we may even be able to find you some additional improvement."

When you offer to be a second set of eyes it helps deepen the relationship and allows them to experience firsthand your service orientation and expertise.

The idea is to start building the relationship even though there is an incumbent. Remember, on average, 52 percent of these prospects are likely to look to switch providers within a year or two. By building the relationship early, you give yourself the inside track for when they do switch. And you can create the impetus for making a switch happen now, not later.

Voicemail—To Leave or Not to Leave

One of the great debates about telephone prospecting is whether or not to leave a voicemail. The arguments against usually include, "No one ever calls back anyway," or, "If I leave a voice mail, I can't keep calling back," or "I can't get my message across in five seconds. Anything longer and they just hit delete."

Successful voicemail formulas follow the same basic format you'd use for a live telephone call, except you have to be really intriguing and more to the point. Please see examples starting on page 177.

PUSH BACK 3: WE'RE ALREADY WORKING WITH SOMEONE

One of the most common push backs is, "We already work with another provider to do this, and they're doing well."

If you're like most salespeople, you politely say, "Thanks for your time. I understand. Have a great day." And you move on to the next prospect, marking this one as a "no" because they're locked up with a competitor.

Buyers Switch Providers Regularly

In our research *How Clients Buy*, we looked at several different industries to gauge a buyer's likelihood to switch to a new provider. We found that unless a buyer is "very satisfied," in rating the current provider (5 out of 5 on the satisfaction scale), they are likely to be open to switching providers. See Figure 13.2.

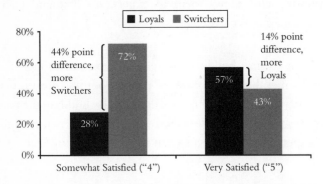

Figure 13.2 Difference in Loyalty by Satisfaction Level

Furthermore, only 48 percent of buyers said they are indeed "very satisfied." That means that in 52 percent of these situations, there's a real opportunity to unseat the incumbent provider and win the business.

Call component	What you say
Name	Tom, this is Jack Fisk calling.
Organization	With Raptor Strategies.
Intrigue to generate interest	**Select one of the approaches to capture attention and generate interest we discussed earlier in this chapter**
Example 1: Best Practices	In looking at your web site, I noticed you were deep in the middle of some major new launches. We've just completed a major benchmark research study to identify the key drivers of cost reduction and speed improvement in clinical trials that I am fairly certain could shed some light . . .
Example 2: Straightforward	I read in the *Chronicle of Higher Education* that you just joined Triton College as their new vice president of development. I'd like to share with you how we recently helped state university increase their fundraising results by an average of 15 percent per campaign . . .
Example 3: New idea	I was just on your web site, and saw a note in a press release that you were looking for any and all ideas on how you can leverage open innovation. I have some ideas from our work I am confident can stimulate your thinking . . .
Example 4: New and different method	In looking at the career opportunities on your web site, I know you have a lot of open sales positions. I want to share with you how we have helped companies like Cisco reduce their ramp-up times for new sales reps by 50 percent and decrease new rep turnover by 15 percent in a breakthrough new way . . .
Example 5: First step	I'm calling to invite you to a private, CEO-only dinner and speaker event at the Copley Plaza in downtown Boston featuring the dean of Boston University Business School . . .

(continued)

Call component	What you say
Example 6: Can you help?	I'm calling because I'm hoping you can help me. We've just completed a major research study with 400 IT directors on trends in intrusion detection and prevention. I'm looking for the person in your IT department who might like to see that research. Can you please call me back at 555-555-5555 or e-mail me at bseller@raptorstrat.com to let me know who that might be?
Call to action	We should talk. I am looking at Wednesday at 2 PM for a 15-minute chat to share this with you. Give me a call at 555-555-5555 or e-mail me at bseller@raptorstrat.com. Looking forward to getting together.

Once you leave a voicemail, you can call again without leaving voicemails. Just because you left a voicemail on Tuesday doesn't mean you can't try them on Thursday, just don't keep leaving messages every day of the week.

If you've left a few voicemails and also a couple of e-mails for someone, try reversing direction, "Tom, it's Jack Fisk. I thought I'd call and leave this last voicemail to see if you'd like to talk about that best practice data for cost containment in your industry. The best companies are employing four distinct strategies and performing 35 percent better than the pack. It's eye-opening, for sure. If I don't hear back from you, I'll assume you're not interested and this will be the last time I'll reach out. If you'd like to talk, give me a call back at . . . or send me an e-mail at . . ."

Overcoming Call Reluctance, Nancy Reagan Style

A study of more than 4,000 salespeople presented at the 2004 Annual Convention of the Southwestern Psychological Association by Behavioral Sciences Research Press and Baylor University's Hankamer School of Business showed that 33 percent of salespeople experienced "career-limiting fear" when making initial contacts with prospects.

The study also showed that 97 percent of the salespeople with call reluctance got over it once they started actually making calls and contacts with people.

In the early 1980s, Nancy Reagan's solution to the drug problem in the United States was, "Just say no." For a few people, this might have been enough, but for the majority a greater effort was clearly needed to effect change. It was probably no easier for an addict to "just say no" as it might have been for a homeless person to "just buy a house." It doesn't work like that.

Great thing about using the telephone: it *does* work just like that.

Our advice to those of you with call reluctance and fear: Start calling. If you can get over the hump of making the first dial, it's more likely you'll make the second. Once you get on a roll, you're more likely to stay on it. In fact, those that do get on a roll often find they didn't set aside enough names to dial when they sat down to call. Taking that first step goes a long way.

Just start calling.[2]

---

[2] Visit www.rainsalestraining.com/booktools to download a cold-calling checklist that will help you plan and secure appointments with prospects by using the phone.

14 | Handling Objections

I do not like green eggs and ham. I do not like them Sam I Am.

—Dr. Seuss

Unless you are fortunate enough to find prospects who completely understand their own needs, recognize the value you provide, agree with the impact of moving ahead, have supportive buy cycles, and prefer you above all others, you will at some point in your rainmaking conversations run into serious objections. Such as:

- "Well, I like what you said, but I don't think it will work here."
- "We are working with someone right now to handle all our needs in that area."
- "Sounds good, but I have a pretty full plate for the foreseeable future."
- "How much? We're talking about buying your software package, not your entire company."
- "I have been talking to some other providers and their numbers are much lower."
- "I prefer to work with someone with more direct experience in our industry."
- "I have always worked with someone local. You guys are 500 miles away."

181

When faced with comments like these, all too many salespeople get flustered, make mistakes, and, in the process, push the buyer and the sale further away.

Worse, salespeople sometimes ignore objections because they have "happy ears." They don't want to hear objections so they block them out, but the objection remains while the sale disappears.

Some sales experts suggest that you deflect, sidestep, rebut, or try to avoid objections altogether. Readymade, canned responses for objections of all types are everywhere:

"I know you like the idea, but *what is the real reason* you won't try this right now? The investment you make is less than what you might spend on a couple rounds of cocktails on a Saturday night! Plus, we have a money-back guarantee."

"I appreciate your need to wait and talk it over, and *here is what I can do*. I can hold this discount for you if you put a good-faith deposit down and let me know your decision within *24 hours*. I am sure your partner/boss is not going to want to miss out on this, and I'm sure that if he were in your shoes *you wouldn't want him to pass up this opportunity either*. Throw down a 10 percent deposit and we'll reserve this special pricing for you, okay?"[1]

Although the snappy comeback and hard close approach may work in impulse-buy situations, the objections that arise in a complex sale require more than a glib retort. In this chapter we outline what objections are and what's behind them, classify types of objections, and then walk you through a five-step process you can employ to win *the right way* when faced with objections. We also pay special attention to money objections, and help you to leverage the advanced technique of uncovering hidden objections.

An *objection* is an explicit expression by a prospect that a barrier exists between the current situation and what he or she needs to satisfy before buying from you. Objections are clear signals that you have more work to do in the selling process.

Yes, objections are barriers, but they are also buying signals. An objection shows that prospects are engaged. They raise objections because

---

[1] Bob Firestone, *Comebacks and Rebuttals*, www.sales-rebuttals.com/?hop=123ebooks.

in the process of weighing the pros and cons *as they perceive them*, they cannot see a path to success around the barrier.[2]

Your objective is to overcome the objection *the right way* and advance toward the sale. To do so, keep in mind:

- *The close begins the relationship*: In transactional selling, where the relationship doesn't matter, sellers are taught to overcome objections at all costs. This does not work for complex products or professional services. If you plow through the objection without addressing it fully, the underlying reason for the objection will come back to haunt you. And, if you handle the objection as if it or the buyer doesn't matter, you lose credibility and trust.

- *Objections often have merit*: The objection may mean you have not fully articulated your value, not uncovered the underlying needs, not provided a key piece of information, not demonstrated your experience, not differentiated from a competitor, have a tough competitor with advantages over you and numerous other missing pieces.

- *Many objections take a process, not a quick answer, to overcome*: The complex sale often has many buyers with diverse buying criteria. Some objections may only need simple clarification on your part, but others may require you to build a strong case for overcoming them.

Four Objection Types

Objections come in many shapes and sizes, but they all boil down to four categories:

1. *No trust*: The buyer has fear, doubt, or misgivings. She may doubt you, your solution, or your company. She may perceive risk and fear loss if the solution doesn't work out.

---

[2]Sometimes objections, such as price objections, are not what they seem. For instance, buyers may feign money objections to get you to lower your price. Our focus is mostly on legitimate buyers with legitimate objections, but keep in mind some buyers will use objections as a negotiating technique to get what they can.

2. *No need*: The prospect does not yet recognize, or does not yet admit, need. There may be a need that *you* see, but until *she* sees it, you won't be able to sell.
3. *No urgency*: She does not yet perceive the burning platform. You've not yet established impact; she does not see the value.
4. *No money*: She communicates that she doesn't have the budget or can't find the funds.

Regardless of the type, you can handle each one by using our Five-Step Objection Handling Process.

The Five-Step Objection Handling Process

When the prospect indicates that he is not ready to buy, he voices an objection. To handle it right and advance the sale, you should:

1. Listen
2. Understand
3. Respond
4. Confirm
5. Continue

Step 1: Listen

Listen fully to the objection. Don't interrupt. Don't anticipate. Fight the urge to respond immediately. By doing so, you give yourself the chance to hear what is on the prospect's mind.

When presented with an objection, it's natural for your defense mechanisms to go up right away. You don't want to veer off course, so you interrupt and anticipate. When you become defensive, your words sound defensive, your body language looks defensive, and you sound combative rather than collaborative.

As soon as somebody says, "I have a few concerns," you know the objections are coming. Take a deep breath. Force yourself to focus and listen.

Step 2: Understand

The stated objection often masks what's really going on. Your charge is to work with your prospect to get to the root cause of what is standing in the way of a favorable decision. Ask permission to learn more, restate the issue, and then ask questions to understand the issue completely. By asking permission to continue, you let the prospect know that you respect his concerns. It also reduces any adversarial dynamic while demonstrating you want to work *with* him to address issues.

The exchange may look something like this:

Prospect: "I don't have time to address this now. I have too many things on my plate."

You: "Do you mind if I ask a few questions about that?" (Permission to continue)

Prospect: "Go ahead."

You: "I hear that you have a lot of other things going on right now and this doesn't appear to be a priority for you. Is that correct?" (Restate)

Prospect: "No. Well, that's not exactly what I meant. It is important, but my resources are stretched to the limit. I can't ask staff to take this on."

You: "So, this is important, but you are having a hard time figuring out how you can get it done without a negative impact on morale by forcing more on to your team's plate?" (Understand)

Prospect: "That is really what it is all about."

Sometimes when you restate, the prospect himself sees the issue more fully. As a result, you get closer to the true source of the objection. But you are not ready to move on yet. Next make sure you have the objection right. Even if the buyer says, "Yes. That's exactly what my issue is," there's often still more to it. In this case, put that objection aside for a moment and ask, "What else?"

- "What else is bothering you?"
- "What else does that affect?"

- "What else is getting in the way of moving forward?"
- "What else is on your mind?"

Often, it is the answer to that last "what else" that contains the biggest barrier to moving the sale forward. But unless you cover all of the other "what else" options, the barriers continue to exist.

If the objection is major, you can also ask "Why?" In this case, you might find yourself ending up in a fairly lengthy problem-solving session, but, depending on the importance of the relationship or the sale, investing your time to work with the prospect to untangle complicated knots can lead you down the path to great success.

Step 3: Respond

Once you have listened and gotten to the bottom of the issue, it's time to respond. Answer honestly and to the point. Long-winded responses quickly sound insincere. As Queen Gertrude opines in Macbeth, "The lady doth protest too much, methinks." Don't overdo it.

Include in your response your resolution to overcome the objection. Describe exactly how you are going to remove the barrier.

You: "Based on what you've shared, your principal concern is that you feel like this might overtax your staff given current projects. But it won't take too much of your time to initiate the project. It's just what happens after that causes the concern."

Prospect: "Exactly."

You: "How much time do you think it will take your staff if you took this on?

Prospect: Well, it's a lot, isn't it? At least two people for 10 hours a week. And then the same amount of time ongoing every week."

You: "I'm glad we're talking about it. You're right, it will take about that for one week, but after that, the average is one person for three hours every other week. If that were the case, do you think you would feel differently?"

Prospect: "Of course. Doing it once is no problem. It was the ongoing commitment that concerned me. Does it really only take an average of one person 1.5 hours a week to keep it all going?"

> **You:** "That's what our other customers report. Would you like to speak with a handful of them and see what their time commitments have actually been? And, of course, you can ask them whatever else you'd like to ask them about the product."
> **Prospect:** "I would."

Step 4: Confirm

Ask whether your answer will satisfy the objection.

"After you speak with a few of our other customers, and you find what you need to find about the time commitment, will that take care of the issue?"

"Yes, it will."

If the buyer still hesitates, don't give up. Most likely you haven't gotten to the final "what else" yet. On the other hand you also don't always want to take yes for an answer immediately. Sometimes prospects say, "Yeah. That works," and you can tell by their body language or tone of voice that they really aren't happy with your proposed solution. They said, "Yeah, sure," but they're thinking, "I don't want to talk about it anymore," or, "I don't care one way or the other because I've moved on to other things."

It's up to you to say, "I hear you, but it really doesn't sound like you completely agree that this is a good resolution. Am I right? Is there something else still concerning you?" By accepting a lukewarm yes, you can end up continuing to work on a sale, perhaps spending significant time on a proposal and presentation, when you still have a major barrier in your way.

Once you get the prospect to confirm with a genuine, excited, "Yes, that will work," you are ready to move on.

Step 5: Continue

When you are comfortable that you have provided an acceptable solution to your prospect's objection, pick up the conversation wherever you left off. Wherever objections surface, follow the five steps to address them, go back to where you were in the RAIN Selling framework, and continue to advance the sale to commitment.

"Getting back to the heart of the conversation after you hear an objection is always tough. I always stress to my people the concept of T, G, B—time, goal, budget. If it comes down to time or money issues, put them aside and go back to the buyer's goal. If you can help them agree that the goal is still important, then you can work with them to find the time and the money."

—Dave Shaby, Senior Vice President of Business Operations, Bright Horizons Family Solutions

When Money Is (Or Appears To Be) the Objection

Money and budget are tricky, and they are almost never what they first appear. When buyers say some version of, "Money is going to be a problem," any of the following reasons could be behind it:

Price Pushback	They Say	They Think
Honest pushback	"That's a lot. Can we do it for less?"	"I just want you to cut the price—I always ask this, and have succeeded in getting price cuts fairly often."
Bluffing	"I don't have the money—we'll need to do it for less."	"I have the money, but I want to see how low I can get you."
Value challenge	"It costs too much. Money is going to be a problem."	"I don't see why we need to spend that much. It doesn't seem worth it."
Competitor pressure	"Your bid isn't as competitive as the others that I received."	It's *true*, and they're looking to understand why. *or* It's *true* and they're looking to use it against you as a bargaining chip. *or* It's *not true*, they're just saying it.

Price Pushback	They Say	They Think
Budget	"Money's a problem because it's not in my budget"	It's *true*, and they'd like to see what they can work out. *or* It's *true* and they're looking to use it against you as a bargaining chip. *or* It's *not true*, they're just saying it.
Reversing direction on you	"Too much money. Call me back if you think there's something you can do."	*They're bluffing* "They'll call me back. I'll get them lower." *or* *They're not bluffing* "I hope they can lower the price so I can actually buy it."
Money issue masks nonmoney problems	"Money is going to be a problem."	"I have multiple issues holding me back, but I'll just say money is the problem right now."

Responding to Money Objections

- *Don't cave.* It can be tempting to respond right away with, "How much can you spend?" or "Let me see if we can lower the price." Don't get anxious and give away the farm. Follow the guidelines outlined earlier in this chapter. Only then will you get to the heart of the issue, and you can find your way around it.
- *Choose your words wisely.* Price pushback doesn't mean that the prospect is challenging your value as a company or person. We've seen many sellers take price pressure personally. It never turns out

well. As much as you might like to respond "You get what you pay for!" or "Those are my prices and it is worth every penny!" there's no glib, pat answer to money objections. Subtlety and patience will serve you better than sharp wit and a snappy response.

- *Don't dismiss the buyer when they push back.* We often hear this from sellers, "If they push back on price, we don't want them! Pushing back on price is an indicator that a customer will be high maintenance or worse down the road." Perhaps this is not the case. Buyers are taught to challenge prices in multiple ways. Just because they challenge you doesn't mean they are bad people or are destined to be bad customers.
- *Focus on value.* Assuming they're FAINT-qualified, prospects can usually find the funds to buy. (If they're not FAINT-qualified, you aren't talking with the right buyer.) By focusing on value first, you can often fix areas you missed earlier in the sale. If value is not the issue—if they see the reason to move forward—you can continue from here to find out what the problem is.
- *Ask, "Which part don't you want?"* Salespeople are tempted to cut prices when they get persistent push back, especially for deals that seem large to them. The logic goes like this, "It's a $120,000 deal, but if we get it, we can get by with $110,000. That would be better than losing the whole thing." Then they cut price. This is a bad precedent to set if repeat business is important at your company. You'll always end up having to play the price-cut game at contract renewal time.

  Instead, when a client is considering a $120,000 deal comprised of five major components, ask her which component she doesn't want. Then review each component. As the customer realizes she wants the whole thing, you don't cut your price. Also, going component by component helps the prospect remember the impact of each piece. All of a sudden the price seems more reasonable.

  You might also find that clients can pick three of the five items at full price because, indeed, their budget or ability to pay is gone or cut, and it's now smaller. You make the sale, and prepare to expand it as soon as you can.
- *Deal with competitor challenge.* When someone says, "I have competitor bids for less," you can acknowledge that other sellers' prices are, indeed, all over the map, and that what you get from one provider isn't necessarily the same as the other. Then ask the buyer, "Is there a

reason you haven't already rewarded them the business yet?" Clients often state why they'd prefer to work with you, and you can leverage those reasons to maintain your price.

- *Don't start talking cost structure.* When buyers don't see why "something costs so much" they often ask what your cost structure is. Imagine, for example, your company is looking to sell $60,000 worth of technology hardware. Some customers will ask, "Well, how did you come up with that price?" The seller then pulls out a cost sheet with how much each piece costs, and how much time it's going to take for installation. Heading down this path is a slippery slope and leads to nickel and diming. If you went to buy a car and asked what the exhaust system cost or how much the dashboard set them back, you would probably get laughed at. In the same vein, you should not lift up the hood simply because someone asked to see.

- *Financing and payment terms.* Many buyers can't buy because of payment terms. Money is an issue *right now,* but if they could pay it over time, they could buy. Many companies have financing support for their products. One security technology company we worked with greatly increased their sales by training their sales force to understand and use leasing to their advantage. Sales shot up once leasing entered the conversation because, as they told us, it negated buyer sticker shock.

Follow these guidelines and you'll overcome all surmountable price objections. Keep in mind you can't overcome them all. If a buyer is bluffing, or simply, "Won't pay that much," there are only a few options you have. You can call the bluffer's bluff and see what happens. Often he'll come back, sometimes he won't. That's how it goes. If the prospect truly can't or won't buy because of money, then, assuming you can't help with financing, it wasn't in the cards anyway.

Handling the Unspoken Objection

Our definition states "An objection is an explicit expression by a prospect that a barrier exists between the current situation and what he or she needs to satisfy before they buy from you." Sometimes, however, an objection may exist but the prospect hasn't explicitly stated it.

If you sense there's something still under the surface, or if you want to nullify an objection before it even comes up and handle it before the prospect says a word,[3] bring it up yourself and make it explicit. Do this, and you can minimize the impact of the objection, overcome it entirely, and often negate a competitor's apparent advantage over you.

Many years ago, we helped someone we know respond to a request for a proposal (RFP) from a commercial bank. At the time, this company's experience in the banking industry was limited, and, in commercial banking, nil. The prospect had noted that commercial banking experience was important, and asked RFP responders to outline their banking background.

Our client knew they were competing against two other firms that had former commercial bankers on their staff and long lists of banking clients. Our client only made it to the final three because someone on the committee knew them, and then the committee liked what they had to say in their proposal. We knew, though, that our client was probably third in a three-horse race, with the disadvantage of industry experience.

Our counsel to our client: Meet the objection head on and neutralize it. Don't leave the meeting until you get your lack of commercial banking experience out on the table. I (John) attended the meeting. Here's how it played out.

We (John and the client, let's call her Sarah) went into see the selection committee . . . 10 very serious bankers. We presented and then had a good give and take discussion with the committee. All was going well, but nobody brought up the commercial banking experience objection.

As we neared the end of the meeting, Sarah said, "I have one question before we leave."

They responded, "Okay. What's that question?"

"Why has nobody asked us about our limited experience in commercial banking?"

They laughed. Somebody took the bait, and said, "What's up with your limited experience in commercial banking?"

Sarah said, "Can you tell me a little bit more about your concern? Why is it important to you?"

---

[3] This is called *procatalepsis*, or *prebuttal*.

They explained they felt like they were a commodity and that the marketing firm they selected had to understand how difficult it is to demonstrate differentiation.

Sarah then asked, "Can you think of any other kind of industry where it's the same?"

Committee reply, "Oh, yeah. Accounting, for sure. They always say, 'we're different' but I never see it."

"A bunch of technology products and services . . . databases, servers, cabling, security!"

"Insurance!"

"Building products!"

"Law firms!"

"Consumer banking, right down the hall!"

"Industrial equipment!"

"Janitorial services!" (Laughs all around.)

To which Sarah said, "Ah, yes. Well, now we're in business. I've worked with many of these industries, and people at my company have worked in all of them. Granted, in the janitorial industry they were staff, not marketers, but now we're going back a few years." (More laughs.)

Our client won the job. She had a few advantages over the other two competitors, but less commercial banking experience. But she wasn't going to let them keep their advantage.

Neither should you. Anticipate and raise objections that may be below the surface. Don't think that just because objections haven't been raised they aren't there. You take a risk when you bring up possible objections (welcome to sales), but if you're not the front-runner by far, the risk is often worth taking. At the same time, you build the relationship with your honesty and openness. Buyers appreciate that.

Many salespeople see objections as a sign of rejection or a call to arms. With this attitude, it is no wonder objections are so often poorly handled. You can, however, overcome the lion's share of objections if you go about it the right way. Just because your buyer says he does not like green eggs and ham, doesn't mean, after some thought and discourse, he might like them on a box, and he might like them with a fox.

15 | Closing Opportunities, Opening Relationships

These aren't the droids you're looking for.

—Obi Wan Kenobi

The closing technique is a convenient whipping boy. Look around and you'll find article after article that starts by pointing out common closing techniques, and then beating them up as manipulative. You'll read things like "You'll be told to close with the 1-2-3 Close, the Assumptive Close, the Daily Cost Close, the Alternative Close, the Ben Franklin Close, the Banana Close, and 101 others."[1]

"Don't use these closing techniques! They demean both you and the buyer."

And they're right . . . for the most part.

---

[1] Yes, these are all real techniques.

If you plan on doing everything you can to help your client succeed (and you should), and you want to make sure your relationship strengthens with every contact (and you do), then don't try to *trick* someone into taking an action. If clients feel tricked, they won't trust you. Not good for you, not good for them, not good for the sale.

The thought of killing trust is anathema to any seller for whom the relationship is important, and love for the closing technique is about as universal as love for speeding tickets, but many sellers throw out the closing baby with the closing-technique bathwater.

There's nothing inherently wrong with closing.

How many times have you felt:

- You understood the client's world, their business issues, their aspirations, and their afflictions.
- You had the right solution for the client's needs—better than your competitors' and better than the other options available to the client.
- You felt a strong connection to the buyer.
- You knew that if the client chose you or your product or service they'd be better for it.
- The impact of using your solution to solve the problem was clear and compelling.
- The value the client would get from working with you was obviously worth the investment.

And then you lost the sale. Perhaps you lost to a competitor, or to "we'll try it internally first," or to "we're just not going to be moving forward at this time."

Regardless of the reason . . . you lost.

Employing a polyester closing technique probably wouldn't have helped, but there's usually *something* you could have done to come out on top.

If you want to win the most sales you need to:

- Understand what closing really is.
- Set the table for success.
- Close with the right actions.

We'll cover each in turn.

The ability to develop and leverage relationships (53.5 percent) tops CSO's list of the most important factors in winning a deal. Executing the entire sales process (24.0 percent) and providing a solid ROI business case (20.3 percent) also appear high in the rankings. How you sell is becoming more important than what you sell.[2]

Understand What Closing Is

Although what you are selling might seem straightforward to you, it's often not straightforward to buyers. They might not know much about you, your technology, your methodology, your competition, your reputation, your solution set, and so on. They're also worried about risks: Will your product do what you say it will do? Is this the right service for us? Will it have the result you say it will? What might go wrong? Are they making the right decision?

The *concept of closing* gets a bad rap because of the manipulative connotation of the *closing technique*. They're not the same.

Definition of Closing—Securing commitment to move forward with a course of action; in our context, typically a sale.

Definition of *Closing Technique*: A manipulation to force a decision. (Jedi mind trick.)

Here are a few things you should know about closing:

- If you're selling complex products and services, what you are selling is, by definition, complex. Buyers need your help to sort it all out.
- Buyers need to make a decision for projects and product purchases or you don't move forward. No decisions, no projects, no sales.
- Buyers all have their own evaluation criteria and processes for making a decision. If you don't satisfy each buyer's criteria and process you won't move forward. Think buying first and selling second (Rainmaker Principle 4).
- If you believe moving forward with you is truly in the buyer's best interest, you should do whatever you can (within the bounds of ethics and integrity) to help them (a) make a decision, and (b) make the best

[2] CSO Insights, "Sales Performance Optimization Report: Sales Execution Analysis," 20.

decision. Not doing so would not be serving your future client, and that's not what you want to be about.

- Closing is risky. Selling is risky. Stepping out your front door in the morning is risky. Although there are some successful sellers whose roles do not require taking positions and making stands, most of us are in the business of giving advice and advocating courses of action (see Rainmaker Principle 8: Set the agenda—be a change agent). If you avoid the risk, and don't take the positions you need to take, you'll lose sales.

If you know it's right for the prospect to move forward, you know you can help, and you have no doubt the solution will work, you should do what you can to close the deal.

Setting the Table for *Close Ready* Deals

Personal relationships and business relationships have a lot in common; some move fast and some move slow. Some work out forever, some for a while, and some never get past the first date.

But every relationship has at least two sides. How it moves forward depends on the wants, requirements, conditions, and options available to each party. The more you satisfy the criteria below, the more your deals are close ready.

- RAIN Selling and selling basics fully addressed:
  — You've built rapport and developed your relationships to the best of your ability with decision makers and influencers in the process.
  — The prospect's aspirations and afflictions are clear.
  — The impact of addressing the buyer's needs is compelling.
  — Your solution will solve the problem.
  — You've painted a picture of the new reality of how the prospect's life will be different and better after she buys from you.
- The buyer is FAINT qualified.
- Buying process is understood and addressed:
  — You know the decision-making process.
  — You know who needs to be involved, and you've involved them at the right time and in the right way.

- You know the overall buying timeline, from first conversation to decision.
- You know the decision-making criteria—their personal criteria as well as their organizational criteria.
- Additional factors that increase your odds:
  - Prospect has indicated a preference toward you and your solution.
  - Buyer has indicated she'll make a decision after receiving your proposal.
  - Buyer is aware of the likely price range and delivery time frame of your solution.
  - Buyer understands her role and responsibilities in working with you.
  - You know the competitive situation, and you've differentiated yourself from the competition.
  - If there's an incumbent, you have explored and established that the prospect is dissatisfied with him.

Will you always be able to address all of the issues above? No. And some factors are more important than others. For example, sometimes you can get buyers to indicate a preference for buying from you and sometimes you can't.

On the other hand, if you don't know if the buyer is the decision maker, and you don't know if she can get the funds to move forward, and you don't know if she has a time frame for moving forward, then the buyer is not nearly close ready.

Line up as many of your ducks in a row as you can before you close.

Close with the Right Actions

The first closing action you must take is to set the table for success and make sure the deal is close ready. Assuming you've set the table, here are the actions you need to take to close the deal, and thus open a new chapter in your relationship.

- *Recommend, don't just present.* Regardless of the situation, the challenges, and the solution, we're all selling one thing: Confidence. Make sure you let the buyer know, "Given everything we've considered, in my estimation this is the best path to move forward." Depending on the situation, you may offer one path only or you may offer options. Whatever you're proposing, recommend one. Your advice is worth taking. Give it. Be a change agent, and set the agenda.

- *Present, don't just send, the proposal.* In-person presentation is best, but live delivery over the phone or web is also a popular option. Don't expect your proposal to continue the sales conversation or close without you.

- *Preempt objections.* You'll need to be able to respond to objections. But first things first: If you can, neutralize objections before the client brings them up. For example, you might say, "If I were in your shoes, I'd consider four ways to tackle this issue. The first way is Option Z. I'd consider it because of reasons A, B and C. But because of your criteria D, E, and F it's really not an option. Here's why." Essentially, you are helping the prospect sort through the pros and cons by bringing up the cons yourself and dealing with them as you go.

- *Indicate you'd like to work with them.* In our *How Clients Buy* benchmark research, buyers reported being turned off much more by underzealous "do not seem to care about working with me" sellers than overzealous "choose me, choose me" sellers. Sellers with integrity are often worried about putting too much pressure on buyers. Take note, however, that buyers might interpret your low-key approach as an I-just-don't-care attitude. Most buyers prefer engaged and passionate sellers.

- *Communicate the next step clearly.* You may have provided a place to sign, but that's not enough. Communicate to the prospect that, "The next step is for you to say, 'let's move forward,' and sign the agreement," and then suggest a time to kick off the engagement or take possession of the product. If you let the opportunity to present next steps float away, that's what might happen to your sale.

- *Push back on put-offs.* If you've presented the solution and the prospect says, "We'll talk it over internally. Can you get back to me in a few weeks?" Your initial reaction might be, "Sure. Will do." Don't capitulate here! It's better to say, "We can certainly talk again, but can you tell me what it is you'll be discussing?" and then continue to probe.

You might find that the prospect has a lingering objection that you need to address. You might find you don't have someone involved in the buying decision who should have been involved. Or you might find your prospect has the authority to go ahead, but a financial buyer needs to sign off. If that's the case, then don't just say you'll follow up in a few weeks—put something on the calendar right then.

Once you accept a put-off you are put in the position of needing to chase the prospect. It also shifts the dynamic to one where you seem to want it more than the prospect does. You have to make sure you're doing everything you can to maintain a peer dynamic and, as well, set actions that advance the sale versus letting it drift along.

- *Help your prospect agree to success versus perfection.* Sometimes the close hangs up because a buyer wants perfection. If you find that a buyer has the mind-set of working on little detail after little detail, let him know you think the best next step is to move forward. You can make some changes on the fly later if needed, and the best path to success is to stop the planning-to-move-forward phase and enter the moving-forward phase.

  You might think, "But pressure like that could kill the trust." Think of it like this: You're a top advisor to a CEO. If you were working with your CEO on an important merger, and she got stuck unnecessarily on a few details and everything ground to a halt while she considered and considered and considered, it would be your duty to advise her that she's not helping herself or her company.

  Its takes some bravery to do this (play to win-win, Rainmaker Principle 1), but—and read this carefully—if it's the *right thing for the client* then you should insert yourself and help her make a decision. Don't discount the possibility that this may even *enhance trust*. Picture the buyer saying, "I am analytical and I need to be more decisive. You helped me move along. Others had the opportunity to do it, but you were the one who did it. We're a good team."[3]

- *Be willing to walk away.* Let's say the prospect pushes on price, pushes for more scope at the same price, or wants you to discount because of the volume of the purchase. Some buyers will continue to do this until you say, "The agreement on the table works for both of us. As it stands, the price is firm as are the deliverables and scope. We can always back up, but I think we've both worked fairly diligently to

---

[3] Visit www.RainSalesTraining.com/booktools for more on the eight buyer personals and how to succeed with them.

come to the best solution for you. If we can agree to the price and the scope I'm confident we'll have success moving forward, but if we can't, then perhaps it's not in the cards."

Sometimes customers don't see the value in the solution and that's why they push price. If this is the case, then the breakdown happened much earlier in the table-setting process. Other times customers simply feel the need to push until you say, "Here's where we are. Let's move forward or move on." Then they're ready.

- *No doesn't always mean no.* If the prospect says no, don't just wilt. This isn't advice to "ask for the sale five times" as you might find in transactional sales; this is about understanding what's going on. Sometimes you can find a buyer who says, "Well, all seemed to be in order, but we just don't think your solution is going to work out for us." Ask why and stay with it until you learn why. You may find something simple was wrong, that he didn't think he needed a component of your offer so he decided to buy from a competitor. Or you didn't communicate something in the proposal that he would actually get as a part of your solution. Often they haven't made a selection yet, and there's still room to turn it around.

  Even if he selected a competitor over you, if you find out who it is and what the competitor is doing, you might find there's still room for you, that the prospect is planning on working with you in another area, or that there's some other option that includes you. It's not uncommon for a prospect to buy from one company only to learn six weeks later that it doesn't work out. If you don't ask, you might miss an opportunity to turn it around.

- *Once you've sold it, stop selling.* We've seen salespeople sell something. The prospect agrees to move forward and then the salesperson keeps talking. "Here's what we'll do. Here's how this often goes. Here are a bunch of things I'll be asking in the first meeting." Only to see the prospect say, "Wow, that brings up about 20 new questions for me. Before I sign I'll have to go back to the office and discuss these with the other stakeholders." Once you get your yes, get a signature and schedule the next steps. Don't sell it and then buy it back.

As you find yourself working toward the close, keep in mind Rainmaker Principle 1, play to win-win. If you keep the buyer's interest firmly in mind, you'll be looking at every possibility during the sales process to help that prospect win. But then you must win the sale, or everybody loses. Don't be afraid to close with purpose if it's the right thing for all involved.

16

What You Need to Know to Sell

Knowledge is the food of the soul.

—Plato

Here's a shocker: The companies that are the best at selling do things differently than those that aren't. If someone asked you to guess the top factors that separate the best sales forces from the average, some obvious choices might be: The best companies hire the best sales reps; they train them well; they pay them well; they motivate and coach them to perform at their best; they retain the top talent.

All reasonable thoughts and worthy goals, but there's one rarely discussed area that separates the best from the rest: sales knowledge. See Figure 16.1.

In an Aberdeen Group research report[1] 472 business-to-business (B2B) firms reported on a variety of sales-related success factors. Twenty-four percent of firms with salespeople who were best-in-class were markedly better in these three areas:

---

[1] Peter Ostrow, Aberdeen Group, "Optimizing Lead-to-Win: Shrinking the Sales Cycle and Focusing Closers on Sealing More Deals" (Aberdeen Group, 2010).

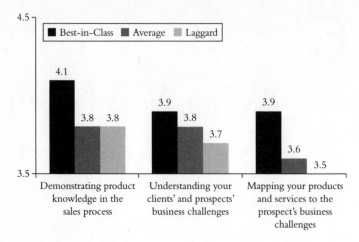

Figure 16.1   Top firms focus on excellence in the core knowledge needed to lead masterful rainmaking conversations.

1. Overall product and service knowledge.
2. Understanding clients' and prospects' business challenges.
3. Mapping their offerings to those challenges.

The top three factors of the firms researched have one thing in common: They all focus on excellence in the core knowledge needed to lead masterful rainmaking conversations.

The findings shine a light on a huge opportunity. Salespeople who are true experts in what they sell—experts in their markets and clients' worlds and experts on how they solve problems—outperform the rest.

Those who aren't experts and who don't have this knowledge run into problems like this:

A salesperson at your technology product company closes a new sale at ACME, Inc. ACME loves how you solved Big Problem A for them. They spent $100,000. They will save $2 million over the next four years. Working together was a joy. Everything went swimmingly.

About three months later, a vice president (VP) at your organization says to the salesperson, "I was just talking to the folks at ACME. Didn't we implement a new product for them a few months ago?" Salesperson: "Yes, we did. It went great. We saved them $2 million by solving Big Problem A."

> VP: "Did you see that Second Problem B existed?"
> Salesperson: "Yes. We looked at it. But my core product area doesn't really address that. Do we have a product that solves that?"
> VP: "Yes. And it's the leading product in the world in that area. For another $100,000, we could have saved ACME another $2 million. Instead, they're working with our biggest competitor now."
> Salesperson: "Well, if I only knew it was that much of an issue. And if I only knew we had products and services in that area, too."
> VP: "Too bad. I only just found out they had Second Problem B myself because our competitor announced the new contract. That should have been our sale."

If this salesperson had the proper product and customer knowledge he would have never missed the opportunity and, indeed, he would have doubled his sale. Rainmakers are sales-knowledge experts; they're fluent in the knowledge they need to sell (Rainmaker Principle 5). If you want to get there yourself, you need to know what rainmakers know.[2]

What Rainmakers Know

Across companies and industries, rainmakers share two traits when it comes to sales knowledge:

1. They know the right things.
2. They know them fluently.

Rainmakers Know the Right Things

All salespeople need to know the same categories of information, regardless of what kinds of products and services they sell. Over the years, we at RAIN Group have identified these categories and have developed the Universal

---

[2] Although they're in the minority, some organizations systematically create sales organizations filled with fluent sales-knowledge experts. If you would like to learn how the leadership at top companies accomplish this, visit www.raingroup.com/booktools and download the paper "How to Build the Expert Sales Force."

Sales Knowledge Framework as a guide to teach salespeople what they need to know to sell.

There are eight essential categories of knowledge you need to sell at your best:

1. *Expectations.* You need to know what you're expected to produce, the actions you're expected to take, and the guidelines to help get you there. This may seem obvious, but less than half of all workers in the United States aren't clear on what they're supposed to do in their jobs.[3] And in sales, expectations are critical. Salespeople need to know, at a minimum:

- What are my goals?
- Should I follow a specific sales process?
- If I'm new, what are my ramp-up expectations? How many sales? How quickly?
- What sales knowledge do you expect me to have?
- How will I be measured (and paid)?
- Along the way, how will I know if I'm succeeding, or if I'm not?
- What does top performance look like?
- Where can I go if I have questions about whether I'm doing the right things?

Whether your company has clearly outlined its expectations of you or if you've set your own goals, you should be well underway here. Remember, rainmakers live by goals (Rainmaker Principle 2). Even if your company is clear about its expectations of you, having your own set of goals and a plan to reach them will put you in the elite class.

2. *Market context and company value proposition.* You need to know the markets you serve backward and forward, including the macro trends in each market, what it's like in your customer's world, the general competitive dynamics of the market, and how your company positions your value to the market.

In *How Clients Buy*,[4] we asked more than 200 buyers about what factors influence their purchase decisions. The one factor that was extremely or

---

[3] Mike Schultz and John Doerr, *Professional Services Marketing* (Hoboken, NJ: John Wiley & Sons, Inc., 2009), 81.

[4] RainToday.com, *How Clients Buy: 2009 Benchmark Report on Professional Services Marketing and Selling from the Client Perspective* (RainToday, 2009).

very important to 90 percent of buyers was "The overall value the provider can deliver." Another 83 percent of buyers said that, "Experience in my industry/business" was extremely or very important. Buyer trust rises significantly (along with sales) when buyers feel like sellers are industry insiders and know how they provide value in the industry.

3. *Categories of common customer needs.* To succeed in sales you have to have a solid understanding of all the possible customer needs you can improve. Even with the most complex products and services, the customer needs can be categorized and labeled, making it easy for you to work systematically to uncover the full range of potential needs. Categorizing needs in this way can make the difference between a master and an average salesperson at uncovering buyer aspirations and afflictions (needs). See Figure 16.2.

In this case, each of the categories highlights the potential needs of a particular type of customer who might buy a particular financial product. What you don't see is that each need has five or six specific needs that comprise the category (see Figure 16.3). You need to know the needs categories and their specifics backward and forward. You can't uncover needs and then connect them to your solutions if you don't know what the needs are in the first place.

4. *Company capabilities as solutions to needs.* It goes without saying that you have to know your products and services deeply, and most companies

Figure 16.2   Sample Customer Needs Model

Need	Capability that Solves the Need	Question to Uncover the Need	Impact on the Customer
• **Category:** Care for others • **Specific need:** Provide adequate retirement income for spouse • **Description:** Clients need to consider ongoing income needs of their spouse if they pass away. Often retirement and by the loss of a spouse can leave survivors financially vulnerable at a time of great stress	ABC Financial Co. *Marketplace Variable Annuity* provides lifetime income for client and spouse, and transfers to spouse should client pass away, providing worry-free lifetime financial security	"You have a number of financial products in place for your retirement together, but have you considered how to provide ongoing lifetime monthly income should one of you survive the other?"	Worry-free lifetime retirement income Financial independence should one spouse survive the other Financial peace of mind at most challenging times

Figure 16.3   Organize Capabilities around the Customer's World—Connect Markets, Customer Needs, and Solutions.

Example: Company solution mapped to specific customer need

focus a significant amount of their training on product knowledge. Product knowledge training rarely does a good job positioning products and services as solutions to customer needs. Positioning company products, services, and overall capabilities as solutions to needs makes it much easier for you to uncover aspirations and afflictions, and analyze where you can make the most impact.

In companies where the organization does not do this for everyone, top sales performers do it for themselves. They have the knowledge they need (Rainmaker Principle 5), and they organize it similarly to what you see in this example, thinking customer needs and buying process first, and selling second (Rainmaker Principle 4).

5. *Competition.* You need to know the details of how and why your company is preferable in specific situations versus the competition. If you don't know the competition, or if you have blinders on when it comes to competition, you'll be vulnerable when selling against them.

6. *Sales strategy, process, tactics, and resources.* When it comes to sales strategy and process, two things need to come together to help you succeed: You need to follow it, and it needs to be a good process.

First, following a sales process impacts performance and success, regardless of the rigor of the process itself.

Second, the better the sales process, the more salespeople sell. CSO Insights categorizes four levels of the sales process: ad hoc, informal, formal, and dynamic. Dynamic processes have much more impact on success than when there is no sales process (ad hoc) or the process is loose (informal).[5]

If you or your company don't have a sales process, put one in place and follow it.

At companies that do have a sales process in place, rainmakers know what it is, follow it,[6] and leverage all of the sales resources available to them.

The popularity of *sales playbooks*—guidelines for how to succeed when faced with specific situations—has been building in recent years. Sales playbooks fit here, and rainmakers know the plays they can run to help them win.

> When we have been the most effective in our history of selling product and watching our campaigns be effective, is when we drill our people the hardest and we know that people go out there with complete knowledge of our products.
>
> —Mike Treske, president, John Hancock Annuities Distribution, John Hancock Wood Logan

7. *Post-sale delivery and service.* You need to know what happens when the sale ends and the customer service begins. In sales conversations prospects almost always have questions about what's next after they buy. Any seeming lack of familiarity with postsale product delivery and service creates buyer doubt.

8. *Account development.* Working closely with number 6, you need to know the strategy for maintaining, deepening, and broadening relationships with customers. If you don't, well, here's shocker number two in this chapter: You won't maintain, deepen, and broaden relationships with customers as well as those who have a strategy.

---

[5] CSO Insights, "2010 Sales Performance Optimization Report: Sales Process Analysis," 20–21.

[6] It's a common perception that the best sales reps are mavericks and only take their own counsel on how to sell. This happens sometimes, but don't confuse this with not following a process! After having studied the seeming madness of elite sales reps, they all follow a process. It may or may not be the one the company lays out for them, but never believe that rainmakers aren't among the most methodical of businesspeople.

These eight categories highlight the types of knowledge that rainmakers need to know. When it comes to sales knowledge, there is one other thing that sets rainmakers apart from the pack . . . how well they know it.

Rainmakers Are Fluent in Sales Knowledge

Think for a minute about what it's like to talk to people at your company who really know their stuff. Ask them a question and they have the right answer right away.

Ask these people a tricky or vague question, and you can tell they know what you're asking about because they ask clarification questions like a physician diagnosing a health problem. They clarify what you're asking, get right to the heart of the issue, and don't waste time on tangents.

This is what it's like speaking with a fluent salesperson. We define sales knowledge fluency as: Fluency = Accuracy + Speed + Breadth and Depth of Knowledge. In a sales context that means that the knowledge salespeople have is correct (accurate). They can apply the correct knowledge without hesitation (speed). And they don't have gaps in their knowledge that hamper their ability to sell (appropriate breadth and depth). See Figure 16.4.

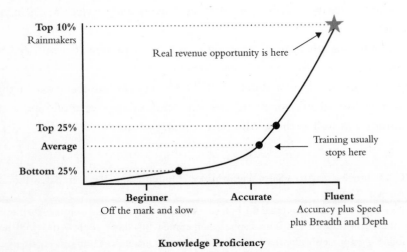

Figure 16.4 Fluency Needed for Maximum Sales Performance.

Most company product knowledge sales training stops at accuracy, leaving salespeople to their own devices to get to fluency. But many never get there.

Let's leave the world of sales for a bit and assume that you are training a financial manager to use a particular spreadsheet feature. It's okay if the manager goes to use that feature, he hesitates for a short time, and then he thinks, "Hmmm, how do I do that again? Let me think . . . Right! Now I remember."

Assume now that you train a salesperson only to accuracy. A prospect asks a question and the salesperson says, "Wait, I know this one. I had training on it. It's . . . it's . . . it's . . ." Even if the salesperson gets the right answer, that five seconds of hesitation damaged his credibility.

If you don't respond immediately when you hear a buying signal, you might miss the sale. If you don't ask the right question at the right time, you miss the opportunity to uncover additional needs and sell the broadest solution set. If you don't have a good response for an objection, the sale will die at the eleventh hour.

Accuracy isn't enough for sales. Product knowledge alone isn't enough for sales. You need fluency: Accuracy + Speed + Breadth and Depth of Knowledge. After all, as Plato told us at the beginning of the chapter, knowledge is the food of the soul.

It's also the food of the sale.

17 | Planning Each Rainmaking Conversation

Eighty percent of success is showing up.

—Woody Allen

Woody Allen's advice is pretty sound for salespeople as well, assuming you show up prepared.

We acknowledge that sometimes you do just have to show up (or—hallelujah—a prospect calls you out of the blue) and you haven't done any preparation for the sales call. It's reasonable to suggest that on occasion sales calls are appropriately deemed *exploratory discussions*—the kind of discussions in which we just talk and see where it goes.

Take this approach in every business development situation, however, and you'll lose a big share of sales that you should have won. Whether you have a $2,000 or a $2 million price point to increase your odds of winning new clients, you still need to do the same basic planning and know the same essential information before your sales calls.

Here are six sales call planning questions you can answer for yourself before every sales call will help prepare you for success.

215

Planning Question 1: What Is the Prospect's Current Situation?

Ask this question to give yourself the lay of the land. Often your goals for the customer, the value you can offer, and your action planning for the rest of the sales call come out of your detailed knowledge of the prospect's situation.

If you find that you don't yet know enough about the situation, ask yourself what research you can do before meeting. Your goals are to be able to move quickly through tactical situational discovery so you don't bore your client in the meeting, and demonstrate that you are the type of professional that does your homework. Make it clear that you will go the extra mile to make sure the client gets the most value out of each contact with you.

Planning Question 2: What Are My Sales Goals for this Prospect?

Different goals will make for different sales conversations. Questions you can ask yourself include:

- Is this the discovery meeting where we get to know each other and build rapport, discuss their needs, and begin to discuss how I might be able to help them?
- Is this a current customer to whom I am introducing a new set of products or services?
- Am I reviewing the results from the previous year with a customer in a meeting where I resell my value so the customer stays loyal?
- Am I looking to cross-sell or up-sell currently available products and services because I see where they can add value for the client?
- Am I trying to supplant a competitor?
- Is this a current client for whom I work in one of their divisions, and I would like to work with the other three divisions?
- Is this a prospect with so much potential that I'd be willing to travel on my dime to five cities to visit her branch outlets and her competitors, and then put together a presentation and value proposition so compelling that she is wowed like she's never been wowed and then resolve to work with me on the spot?

Whatever your sales goals for this prospect or client, make certain you are as clear as possible about what those goals are before the actual meeting.

Planning Question 3: What Is My Desired Next Outcome?

Sounds simple enough, but this question is so often overlooked by sales professionals before they meet with prospects. Our advice: If you don't know what you want to get out of your meeting, don't get out of the (proverbial) car. Among your possible outcomes:

- I want to leave with a promise for an introduction to the other decision makers.
- I want to find out what caused the service breakdown in the past, and get the client to reconsider us in the future.
- I want to clarify exactly what the client is trying to do with his new product launch and see where we can be of value so we can move to proposal.
- I want to review our latest proposal and get commitment to move ahead.

Just make sure you start your sales call planning process early enough, so you have time to investigate anything you need to do in order to prepare.

Planning Question 4: What Are My Relative Strengths?

In every sales situation, various forces are working in your favor. Know what these forces are for each client or prospect situation so that you can leverage them.

Some examples of strengths that can help you are:

- We have a relationship with a board member who has the CEO's ear.
- One of our offices is five miles from the prospect's main plant.
- We know the client is unhappy with her current provider. And we know why.
- The prospects attended a training program our president conducted and wrote a great evaluation.

- The current CFO worked at our firm for three years and still maintains contact with two of our division leaders.

The more specific you can be for the particular situation, the better. It might be a general advantage that you are a well-known leader in your field with a good reputation, but it's a better advantage to know against whom you are selling (if anyone), whether or not you and the potential customer went to the same college, if you've been particularly successful in this industry versus your competitor, or any other specifics that might be working in your favor.

Planning Question 5: What Are My Relative Vulnerabilities?

This is the corollary to Planning Question 4. Maybe you have less experience than the competition. Maybe another company is the incumbent service provider and you are the challenger. Maybe your product doesn't dominate the competition. Knowing what your relative vulnerabilities are will allow you to prepare in advance to either turn them into advantages or, at least, diminish them as vulnerabilities.

Perhaps your competitors have more experience in the industry, their reputation is quite good, and they've been doing this forever. If you prepare for this vulnerability, you can say:

"Yes, they do have a lot of experience in the industry as this is their only focus. Because our focus is broader, we bring knowledge from outside the industry that has been incredibly valuable to our other clients. Did you know that in the XYZ Company in a different industry they designed their divisions like this . . . last year and got a 7 percent cost savings after implementation? Maybe it will apply to your company. We can look into it together, if you'd like."

With good preparation and call planning, you can have your responses to objections and tough questions at the ready when you need them.

Planning Question 6: What Actions Do I Need to Take Before the Next Call?

We all have to-do lists that help us get done what we need to get done. By taking the time to answer questions 1 through 5, your sales call planning to-do list will be as good as it possibly can be because your actions will be:

- Informed by the knowledge of your client's situation.
- Guided by your goals for the client from a business development perspective.
- Built to help you achieve your desired outcomes.
- Planned with the knowledge of your relative strengths and vulnerabilities in this particular business development situation.

Maybe for Woody Allen 80 percent of success in life is just showing up. But the most successful salespeople we've seen over the years show up prepared.

Visit www.rainsalestraining.com/booktools to download the Sales Call Planner tool and example.

18

How to Kill a Sales Conversation

My roommate got a pet elephant. Then it got lost. It's in the apartment somewhere.

—Steven Wright

Have you ever watched someone head down a path in a conversation where you knew—you just knew—that the person was about to self-destruct and there was nothing you could do to help?

Perhaps it was going well for a while and then took a turn for the worse, and perhaps he lost the other person at hello. Either way, the conversation mistakes he made were about as obvious to you as an elephant hiding in the bathroom behind the toothbrush, but, for whatever reason, the perpetrator of conversation destruction couldn't see the elephant.

When sales conversations die, they rarely go out with an explosion. More often they expire with a whimper. It doesn't matter if the conversation killer was the size of an elephant or a gnat, there was a sale that could have been made, an objection that could have been overcome, or a price point that could have been achieved but wasn't, the failure is usually somewhere in the conversation.

We've categorized the conversation killers into four categories:

1. Killers that make you dead on arrival.
2. Killers hiding in the open.
3. Killers waiting to ambush you.
4. Killers you never see that kill in the dark.

We cover each in turn, but before we do, it's important to note that if you've been following the advice throughout *Rainmaking Conversations*, for the most part you already know how to avoid these pitfalls. However, over the years we've observed that even when given all the information people need on the "right" things to say and do, it still helps to know what all the "wrong" things sound like. That is, it makes sense to people once they see what not to do, and it helps their sales conversation trains stay on the tracks.

Killers that Make You Dead on Arrival

Regardless of how good your sales conversation skills might be, let any of the following killers sneak in and your chances of running a great conversation are slim even before you show up to the meeting.

Lack of preparation: Heading into a meeting without learning what you should learn about a company, knowing what you want to get out of the meeting, knowing who you're meeting with, and being ready for what might happen.

Effect: You can't hold an effective conversation on many fronts. Whatever you say demonstrates your unpreparedness. Prospect dismisses you, moves on to find more credible and professional options.

Fix: See Chapter 17, Planning Each Rainmaking Conversation.

Not establishing your competence: Seeming to lack the knowledge and insight that you should have.

Effect: Can't or don't ask incisive questions, stay on topic, discuss specifics, make relevant comments, suggest ideas that are on-target, or provide insight. Prospect dismisses you as not likely to be able to help them. At best, you don't stand out. More often, creates mistrust of your professional capabilities, transfers same doubt onto your company.

Fix: See Chapter 16. See all chapters on RAIN Selling, especially balancing advocacy and inquiry.

Professionalism issues: Showing up late, forgetting meetings, creating scheduling snafus, dressing inappropriately, or using bad language.

Effect: At first, prospect is slightly taken aback. Conversations start off on a bad foot, and you're playing defense from the get-go. You'll miss some meetings and not be able to reschedule. More than one of any of these issues and the prospect thinks you're a dope.

Fix: Be on time. Confirm meetings. Dress for success. Keep language appropriate. Don't be a dope.

Setting up adversarial dynamic: Thinking of prospects as the enemy, people to trick, or seeking to win at their expense.

Effect: Inability to build trust. Build trust by faking it and eventually get found out for something adversarial or sneaky and you kill trust forever.

Fix: Genuinely try to help the prospect win, and you will, too. Rainmaker Principle 1: Play to win-win.

Failure to prospect: Not putting new conversations in the pipeline all the time.

Effect: Leads to conversation CPR (always trying to resuscitate and breathe life into dying prospect situations, or situations that have no chance at life). Not enough new prospects and you'll focus your conversations on the most desirable of the undesirable because there's no one better at the dance.

Fix: Rainmaker Principle 6: Create new conversations every day. See Chapter 13.

Lack of follow-up: Not staying on top of customers and worthwhile prospects in your pipeline.

Effect: Stalls at all levels. Deterioration of relationship strength and conversation richness. Missed windows of opportunities. Passage of time distracts otherwise interested prospects. You and your solutions fall off their radar screens. Lost sales to competitors who are following up. Competitors selling to customers to whom you are not paying enough attention.

Fix: Follow up in order of importance of relationships and sales prospects. Keep good records and tracking of who needs follow up. Schedule discussions with important relationships regularly. Step back and ask yourself in your sales-planning sessions what the order of priorities are for follow-up and then take action. Add more resources to help you follow up if you can't keep up yourself with high value prospects and customers.

Playing to sort-of win: Not giving it your all. Not devoting all the energy and attention to doing what you must to win.

Effect: Problems in all areas. Lack of knowledge, lack of follow-up, prospecting avoidance, relationship deterioration, making your competitors look better. Conversations weaken at all phases.

Fix: Rainmaker Principle 1: Play to win-win. Check your passion, desire, and commitment levels. Get back to goal setting. Turn the heat back up on reaching success by devoting yourself to excellence (Chapter 3, Goal and Action Planning).

Killers Hiding in the Open

The conversation killers we're about to outline are obvious (thus the hiding in the open part). We apologize in advance for stating things that you probably know, but *knowing* something is a mistake and *avoiding* it are two different things.

Obvious or not, these mistakes are made daily, and the cost of making them is as painful and problematic as any other conversation killer.

Lack of rapport: Inability to make a connection with the prospect. For phone sales especially, inability to make a quick connection with buyers. Can happen for many reasons, from inappropriate language, dullness, failure to capture attention, inability to break early tension, not smiling or seeming warm, arrogance or subservience, insincerity, inappropriate dress, not listening, veering inappropriately off topic, and so on.

Effect: Inability to get past pleasantries and into the meat of sales conversation. Inability to get back in touch with people for a second meeting. Buyers who stick with you feel like they're fighting an uphill battle because they may pursue buying despite needing to deal with you.

Fix. See Chapter 13 on prospecting to create early rapport and Chapter 5 on building rapport in general.

Failure to demonstrate understanding: Doubt in prospect's mind as to whether you really get what's going on.

Effect: Doubt in prospect's mind that what you suggest as a solution will really work. Little chance that, if you have to work with the prospect on an ongoing basis to solve problems, you will win the deal.

Fix: Assuming you do understand all facets of what's going on (reread all sections on RAIN Selling to help you get there), confirm understanding verbally and in writing.

Talking too much: Taking up too much air time.

Effect: Lack of connection. Inability to understand situation fully. Loss of interest by the prospect.

Fix: Balance advocacy and inquiry (Chapter 6).

Not listening: Appearing to buyer as if you did not pay attention to what they said.

Effect: Complete conversation destruction.

Fix: First, listen actively. Second, demonstrate that you are listening. Keep eye contact, maintain active posture, nod where appropriate, and don't cut the prospect off when he's speaking. Third, confirm with buyer what your understanding is so he sees that you have listened.

Not advocating or setting an agenda: Not providing thoughts and ideas, insights, or recommendations on how to move forward.

Effect: Buyer has no reason to believe you'll be a partner in crafting solutions, in solving problems as you work together, and in creating more value than simply selling what you're selling. Buyers feel like they're still driving the bus when they'd like to see others take responsibility for ideas, direction setting, and action. Any action by your competitors in this area will draw buyers to them, not you. Assuming similar technical competence, you'll lose to competitors that buyers believe will be more valuable to their teams.

Fix: Take a position. Take a risk. Share thoughts. Put forth ideas. Drive the conversation forward. Rainmaker Principle 8: Set the agenda, be a change agent.

Not learning the buying process: Not understanding the details of how a purchase decision will be made with a particular prospect.

Effect: Effects are numerous, including not involving the right buyers, being too late or too early with proposals, not fulfilling purchase needs of the client and losing on technicalities, not setting yourself apart with your value at every buying stage.

Fix: Uncover and confirm the buying process. Rainmaker Principle 4: Think buying first, selling second.

Lack of communication of impact: Buyers don't understand, don't believe, or don't fully appreciate the impact buying from you will have on their success.

Effect: Lack of urgency kills sales. Stalls. Price pressure and objections you could have avoided. Competitor does a better job and wins.

Fix: Establish impact, communicate impact, and confirm impact.

Lack of clear new reality: Buyers don't see the before-and-after picture. Don't know what's going to happen after they buy from you.

Effect: Difficulty seeing the impact, difficulty explaining it to others, lack of connection to the process, diminished desire for the end result.

Fix: Follow the advice in Chapter 8 to establish new reality.

Not establishing trust: Buyer doubts your motives, doubts your competence, doubts your reliability, or doesn't feel connected enough to you to get too close.

Effect: Effects range from hesitance to work with you, never being willing to work with you, and actively seeking to ruin your reputation because you burned them.

Fix: Follow advice in Chapter 5 to establish trust.

Killers Waiting to Ambush You

Killers waiting to ambush you are things that you do (or forget to do) in the sales process that—although they seem small—can kill conversations and, in turn, kill sales.

We describe each conversation and ambush, but we don't outline specific fixes for these. The fix for each one is simply to avoid the problem. Where appropriate, we note where you can learn more in different sections of *Rainmaking Conversations*.

Not involving a key buyer in the process. Leaving out key buyers who you never knew would even have a say will cause you to lose the sale when someone says no, or you can't get a yes because a key buyer was not involved in the buying process appropriately, doesn't feel connected to the solution, doesn't appreciate the impact, and so on.

No involvement, no investment, no sale. If buyers don't feel like they're part of the process, and if they don't have to invest time, money, or psychic energy into solving the problem, then they will not feel as connected as they should to moving forward. The more effort buyers expend in the process of buying, the more connected they are to seeing it through.

Accepting put-offs and allowing attention shifts. Time kills sales. The more time that goes by, the better the chance that purchasing inertia will take hold. The old saw "strike while the iron is hot" is as true today as it ever was.

Peer dynamic imbalance. Buyers who see sellers as peers, and buying situations where the buyer is as interested in the sale as much as the seller, are more likely to yield sales. If you are overselling and the buyer is back on their heels, or underselling while the buyer is pushing but you seem disinterested, you will lose sales. Same if buyers believe you to be subservient to them. Your job is to help, and you can have service orientation, but that doesn't make buyers more senior to you, or that their time is worth more than yours. Don't err on the side of arrogance, though. Many people, when gearing up to talk to senior decision makers, prep themselves by puffing out their chests and trying to sound tough. That doesn't work well.

Going to proposal too early. Trying to close a sale before all of the buying criteria have been met can kill conversations because you send the proposal and then the buyer disappears. Going to proposal too early can also put the focus too much on price because you haven't yet established what you need to establish to make the sale close-ready.

Not taking notes. Not taking notes can cause you to forget important details, and can communicate to the buyer that you're not listening, not taking the situation seriously, and that you're not detail-oriented.

Asking about budget inappropriately. You'll find sales tip after sales tip that will tell you to ask for a budget, but asking this question at the wrong time, in the wrong way, or sometimes even at all can trap you and send a sales conversation down the wrong path.

Taking an ocean voyage. You can kill a sales conversation if you go off on irrelevant tangents. (Yes, there are relevant tangents, like when you're talking about your recent vacation as you build a relationship.) Unless you know where you're going and why, stay on target.

Giving up too early. When some prospects say no or don't respond to a voice mail or e-mail, they may be interested but busy that day. They may always say no a few times before they say yes. Perhaps they're testing you to see how interested you are in pursuing them. It often takes multiple attempts to get through to prospects, multiple attempts to move a stalled sale forward, and overcoming multiple objections to make a sale.

Killers You Never See that Kill in the Dark

Sales expert Dave Kurlan has been writing about hidden weaknesses that hold salespeople back for years. He classifies the five major hidden weaknesses as:

1. Tendency to get emotionally involved.
2. Need for approval.
3. Nonsupportive buy cycle.
4. Money discomfort.
5. Self-limiting record collection.

Each one of these hidden weaknesses lurks in the dark, killing sales conversations every day. Unlike killers hiding in the open and killers that spring out of the bushes to ambush you, these ninja hidden killers kill sales conversations in ways that the seller might never notice happening.

If you want to catch a ninja, the first thing you have to do is know he's out there and how he operates. The second thing you have to do is shine light into dark corners and find out where he's hiding and how he plans to make his move. Let's start by taking a look at what these hidden killers are and what they do.

Tendency to Get Emotionally Involved

Salespeople who have a tendency to get emotionally involved lose their focus when prospects throw them a curveball. The curveball could be a price objection, a stall in the process, introduction of a competitor late in the game, a challenge to something the salesperson said, or virtually anything that can throw sellers off their game.

When thrown a curveball, some salespeople stop listening to the client, and either start thinking to themselves about what to do next, or lose control of the conversation because they get hyped up. The conversation veers down a bad path because sellers start missing things.

Need for Approval

Salespeople who have a need for approval avoid asking tough questions when they think those questions might negatively affect their relationship, find themselves avoiding confrontation, have call reluctance, and are afraid of the word no. It's helpful when salespeople are likeable, but it's not helpful when their need to be liked outweighs their need to be respected and helpful to customers and successful at selling.

Let's say a prospect says, "It's not on the radar right now, can you call me back in three months?"

The salesperson with a need for approval might say, "Sounds good. Will do." and then schedule a time to call the prospect back in three months.

The salesperson without a need for approval might say, "I'm curious to know what is on your radar screen right now?" After the prospect answers, the salesperson might see that the prospect is simply not aware that she can, and should, help right now.

The salesperson then might say, "So you're trying to get this, this, and this because your goal is XYZ. [Prospect confirms.] If I may, I'd like to offer a few thoughts. The first two areas you're approaching seem right on target, but I question whether pursuing the third will actually help you. I've seen a few companies approach it like that and it never comes out well."

The prospect then says, "Oh, really? How so?"

The salesperson says, "Well, if you have 30 minutes or so, I can walk you through a few things you might find helpful. We've seen a few different approaches that are actually working quite well."

Prospect: "Okay. How about Thursday at . . ."

Because she was not afraid to push back and then point out where the prospect was approaching something in a less-than-effective way, she got back on the radar with no three-month wait.

Nonsupportive Buy Cycle

Imagine this: You sell TVs at a major electronics store. A buyer walks in and says, "We just moved to a new house and need a flat-screen TV and entertainment system for our living room. What do you recommend?"

You ask a few questions to determine the buyer's needs and preferences, and say, "Well, I'd suggest a premium 62-inch LCD with XYZ resolution. I'd also suggest the following Blu-ray player, game system, receiver, wires and components, premium remote control, and our platinum install program."

The buyer then asks a few questions about features, whether the system is good quality, and what the benefits are of buying from you. He asks you for a price.

You let him know, "It's $13,500."

He pulls out a credit card.

A second buyer comes in, and when you see him you want to roll your eyes. He's been in 12 times, you know he's been to multiple other stores, has done all his Internet research on prices and rebates, and has been badgering you about taking off a few hundred here and a few hundred there. When your sales manager adjusted the price a few weeks ago and gave him a great deal, he then took that price to someone else to see how low he could get that store to go. He starts off with, "I'm still not ready, but I have a few more questions."

The first buyer knows what he wants, is ready to buy when he finds what he wants, makes a decision, and then doesn't push price.

The second buyer is indecisive, price conscious, needs to explore all the options, needs sellers to educate him, thinks everything is negotiable, and still may not make a decision.

A *buy cycle* refers to the way a person makes major purchases for themselves. If someone has a nonsupportive buy cycle, it means that the way they make major buying decisions for their own purchases negatively affects their ability to succeed in selling. The reason is that sellers who have a nonsupportive buy cycle relate to and support the behavior of the buying habits of the second buyer in the example.

They say things like, "I understand, you want the best deal. I would, too. Let's talk. What would you like to know?" They answer questions, teach about the technology, ask more questions about needs, and so on. When buyers ask more questions about price, they check back with their boss again or say, "Let me sharpen the pencil and see what I can do."

A seller with a supportive buy cycle doesn't go here. First, he wouldn't have allowed the person to keep pushing and pushing on price. Early in the conversation, he would say something like, "We offer the best install service, the best refund policies, top-of-the-line technology, and the best customer service should problems arise. If you are looking for the lowest price, we're probably not the best option for you."

Even if the store explicitly competes on price, this salesperson will say something like, "If you bring the competitor pricing given the same components and service we'll match it, but in my experience, what you're getting at other places is rarely the same," and then focus on value delivered versus price. Should the buyer persist with pushing the price, the seller will often politely discontinue the conversation.

Nonsupportive Buy Cycle Lowers Price Unnecessarily

Several years ago we were listening to a salesperson at a leadership consulting firm sell a leadership training program to a major company. After several months of working through the buying process, at the end of the meeting where the buyer gave conceptual agreement to move forward, he said, "What's the fee going to be?"

The seller, having done a great job getting to the point where the deal was almost closed, said, "It's going to be $175,000, but if that's too much, we can do it for $150,000, unless that's too much, then I'll have to go back and see what I can do."

The seller with the obvious nonsupportive buy cycle always bought with price in mind, so he simply expected the buyer wanted the same.

The buyer said to us later, "I was ready to sign at $175,000. Happy you offered to do it for $135,000 in the end, though."

Even when faced with a good buyer, a seller with a nonsupportive buy cycle can yank profit out of any sale.

You might be thinking to yourself, "You might lose a sale, though." That's fine. Rarely do companies want to compete on price or succeed because they do.

If your company is like most, the more common company line is, "We're actually a higher-priced option than many, but that's for a reason: We offer more value because of . . ." Getting trapped in the price discussion is not a good place to go. Sellers with nonsupportive buy cycles get stuck all too often.

Although you can see Chapter 14 for more on selling value and overcoming price objections, knowing how to do it and actually doing it if you have a nonsupportive buy cycle is not the same thing. You have to fight the urge to support the challenging buyer behavior.

Money Discomfort

It's common in the consulting, law, technology, and marketing industries to sell monthly retainers to clients. We at RAIN Group have had the chance to analyze the sales practices of so many companies. One thing always stands out to us: Some people at a given firm will regularly sell retainers five times the size of others at the same firm. Same services, same market, same value, same territory, and one sells $10,000 per month retainers while the other sells $50,000 per month. We've also seen people who sell $50,000 deals regularly where, again, for the same company and same product and service set, someone else regularly sells $500,000 deals.

This difference often has to do with money discomfort. Money discomfort comes in two flavors: general discomfort talking about money, and money ceiling, where discussing money over a certain amount becomes uncomfortable.

Money discomfort generally starts when people are young. Young Sally says to dad, "How much money do you make?" Or "That bike is $1,399.50. Can you give me that so I can buy the bike?" Or "I asked Jimmy's dad how much his car costs."

This line of commentary by a child is often met with a lecture about how it's impolite to talk about money. Often the reaction by parents is much firmer and makes it quite clear to the young child that money is not something to be discussed, especially with strangers. Regardless of where the discomfort starts, it hurts sales. For those who have a money ceiling, they don't feel comfortable in what, to them, is a high-stakes money discussion. So, they often don't end up there, and they don't succeed even when they do.

In both situations, whether it's general money discomfort or money ceiling, when it comes time for the seller to talk about money, it can derail the sale.

Prospect, "This sounds good in concept. Before we move to the next step in the process here, can you give me a range of what something like this is going to cost?"

Seller without money discomfort, "It's going to be between $20,000 and $40,000."

Seller with money discomfort, "Well, umm, sure. One thing first though: I know it's going to sound like a lot of money . . . sort of because it is . . . but in the end I'm sure you'll see that we're worth it. The budget amount you'll have to commit as an investment can range from $20,000 on the low side . . . sounds funny calling that low . . . and $40,000 on the high side. Do you think that sounds good, or are we too high?"

Even if it's a phone call, from the other side of the phone the buyer can literally see the seller squirming in his seat talking about the dollars. This causes the buyer to wonder:

- Is this worth it?
- What's wrong here?
- This is worth it. I bet I can get it for less. They're showing price weakness from the get go.
- Is this person serious? That's short money. Ugh . . . I'm dealing with another junior person.
- Is this person serious? That's short money. Ugh . . . I should probably head upstream to a higher-tiered firm as I think we might be out of their league, and we need bigger thinkers.

While the buyers are busy wondering about the price because you focused all of your nervous energy there, what they stop wondering about is the value. Once this starts going on in their heads, the sales conversation train is headed off the track.

Self-Limiting Record Collection

When describing why people behave how they behave, psychologists are fond of a concept called *scripts* or *schema*. They contend that people do not think about most everyday situations. They simply react, and there's no need for what they call *effortful processing*. These scripts are preconceived ideas and mental frameworks people have about themselves. Whether they know it or not (usually not) these scripts drive their behavior.

You can also think of scripts as little bits of songs that people sing to themselves in their head . . . a record collection so to speak.

When records play in salespeople's heads, they can either help or hinder the sales cause. We refer to those songs that hinder as self-limiting records. For example, salespeople might say to themselves:

- I'm not comfortable talking to company presidents; they're not my peers.

- My sales cycle is long, and I can't shorten it.
- The economy is down and my prospects don't have much money.
- I can't sell without great sales collateral.
- Talking about money is uncomfortable.
- My product is very difficult to sell.
- Once a request for proposal (RFP) is issued, you can't really affect the specifications.
- If they have a current vendor and they say they're happy, I can't sell to them.
- I don't like cold calling.
- I don't have time to prospect.

Any one of these can negatively affect sales conversations and sales success. If you aren't comfortable talking to company presidents, and if they are your buyers, they'll sense it in your conversations and dismiss you. If you think you can't shorten your sales cycle, you'll never have an effective conversation with buyers geared to increase their urgency, or move a decision along faster. If you think you can't affect buying criteria after an RFP is issued, you won't pursue showing the decision maker a better way to pursue his goals and set yourself apart. If you don't feel like you have time to prospect, you won't, and your pipeline will suffer.

When we evaluate salespeople with our Rainmaker Assessment Instrument, we can uncover more than 60 self-limiting records. If they're present, they're affecting sales conversations, and not in a good way.

I've Met the Enemy, and It's Me, I Think . . .

With any of these five hidden killers, the toughest part is figuring out whether or not you bring them around with you from sales conversation to sales conversation. When we share the hidden killers with people, we usually get three reactions:

1. Too many of them ring true! I'm guilty, now how do we fix them?
2. These don't sound like me. I don't have these issues. Let's move on.
3. These don't sound like me, but they sound like everyone else around here! How do we get them to see it?

The problem with the first two reactions is that what you think is true about yourself and what is really true about yourself are usually two different things.

Chris Argyris, professor emeritus at Harvard Business School and thought leader at Monitor Group, is known for his breakthrough work in the area of human behavior, including writing about "Espoused Theory" versus "Theory in Use."

He says that people hold two types of ideas in their heads about what drives them. The first is espoused theory, the one that they actually believe about themselves and how they behave in certain situations. The second is theory in use, or the one they actually use.

According to Argyris, in everyday situations the espoused theory and the theory in use are often the same. That is, what people think they do and what they actually do are aligned.

But when it comes to situations that involve stress, pressure, potential embarrassment, complexity, or threat he says that the espoused theory and the theory in use are rarely the same. "People become skillfully blind about the inconsistency between their espoused theories and their theory in use. They may become aware of it afterwards, but while they're producing the behavior they are rarely aware, and the end result is that our behavior is often less effective than it could be."[1]

In other words, it's difficult to assess whether you have any of these weaknesses simply by asking, "What do I think is true?" because you only get your espoused theory. If you want to find out what's true about yourself, use a validated sales evaluation instrument and find out what's really going on.

Rainmaker Principle 10 tells us that we need to assess ourselves, get feedback, and improve consistently. Take this principle seriously and remove the killers in your sales conversations, and the only elephant in the room will be the big signed contract for new business that you bring back to the office.

---

[1] Chris Argyris in *Rotman* magazine, Winter 2008, p. 12.

19 | Putting RAIN in Your Forecast

Rain! Whose soft architectural hands have power to cut stones, and chisel to shapes of grandeur the very mountains.

—Henry Ward Beecher

Thank you for taking the time and effort to read *Rainmaking Conversations*. It was a labor of love for us. We hope you found it as worthwhile to read as we found it enjoyable to write.

Now it is up to you.

You are the only person who can determine your success. Just as you need buyers to take ownership of their decisions and agendas, it is up to you to take ownership of your actions and do all you can to make all your sales conversations bear fruit.

No excuses.

Envisioning your own success is a great first step in a journey. We leave you with one last exercise to get you off and running. Before we do, we'd like to remind you to visit www.rainsalestraining.com/booktools where you can download additional content and tools, and log in to your free RAIN Selling online learning lessons that accompany this book.

Now, time to visualize your own New Reality.

Imagine it's three years from today. You are reading the *Wall Street Journal*. On the front page is a rags-to-riches article . . . about you! This glowing article shares how you transcended where you were, fulfilled your potential, and became the rainmaker you knew you could be.

What does it say? How did you do it? What were the defining moments? How does it feel? Those in the business world who haven't made it yet want to know.

As you write your story, keep in mind the 10 rainmaker principles that will guide your path to rainmaking success:

1. Play to win-win.
2. Live by goals.
3. Take action.
4. Think buying first, selling second.
5. Be a fluent expert.
6. Create new conversations every day.
7. Lead masterful rainmaking conversations.
8. Set the agenda; be a change agent.
9. Be brave.
10. Assess yourself, get feedback, and improve continuously.

To give you a little guidance, we have started and finished the article for you. Your job: Fill in the middle:

Dateline (Three Years from Today)—[Your name] claims [he/she] wasn't at the top of [his/her] game at selling yet, but three years to the day after deciding to become a rainmaker [your name], has created a new standard of sales success.

"I realized I needed to develop my sales skills, get out there, and make it happen," [your name] remembers thinking. "Here's what happened, how I got here, and what my life is like now.

[Your story goes here]

"And I guess, the rest is history," [your name] said with a smile. A smile that says to us subtly: Rainmakers have it good.

Now, go out and make it RAIN.

Appendix and Online Resources

Chapter 2 The Most Important Conversation You'll Ever Have

Regardless of what your answers are, the first thing you have to know is, "Am I willing to look?" Assuming the answer is yes, and you'd like to explore further, visit www.rainsalestraining.com/booktools for more insight.

Chapter 3 Goal and Action Planning: Making the Most of RAIN

Visit www.rainsalestraining.com/booktools for a list of 39 planning questions, and tools to help you plan your specific sales activities.

Getting Specific with Sales Planning

Sales is an ongoing process, so it is easy to get discouraged if the only measurement of success along the way is when you win a new deal or achieve your annual target. In a complex products and service sales cycle, these successes can seem to take forever.

The success you measure on your journey can and should include interim milestones, such as number of new conversations generated, number of qualified prospects added to the mix, and number of referral introductions.

As you think about acquiring new business, you'll want to keep tabs on at least the following metrics:

- New conversations generated.
- Qualified opportunities.
- Customers won.
- Average revenue per engagement.
- Revenue generated.

Depending on your sales process there could be even more, such as:

- Profit margins per deal and overall.
- Target account status.
- New appointments set.
- Relationship status and activities.
- Length of sales cycle.
- Number of meetings required to close.
- Cost per sales call and revenue per sales call.
- Account retention.
- Sales team progress toward goals, as a group and individually.
- Profitability by sales person.
- Average account size.

Here's an example of a few of the most basic:

Targets for April

Category	Specific Metric
New conversations needed	20
Opportunities needed	10
Qualified opportunities needed	5
Closes needed	3
Average revenue per customer	$20,000
Revenue generated from new opportunities	**$60,000**

Targets for April

Category	Specific Metric
New conversations needed	
Opportunities needed	
Qualified opportunities needed	
Closes needed	
Average revenue per customer	
Revenue generated from new opportunities	

See below for an example of how to figure out how you can reach the milestones in your sales process.

The end outcome you are looking for is X customers closed over the course of Y time frame. However, you need to set measures that add up to your end goal.

Milestones	Date
Example: Set 48 proactive new sales meetings as an outcome of the actions of this plan	4 per month for each month of the year
Example: Conduct 12 in-depth conversations that come from other sources such as speeches, seminars, web, referrals, and current and recent clients	1 per month for each month of the year
Total: 60 initial meetings	

To help you figure out the various factors you need in place to reach your goals, visit www.rainsalestraining.com/booktools to download the Marketing and Sales Funnel Analysis Tool. This tool is an Excel spreadsheet built to help you:

- Plan your revenue.
- Understand what you need to do in your prospect efforts.
- Determine where you might need to invest and improve (e.g., sales training, lead generation, customer referral programs).
- Calculate the lifetime revenue of your customers.

- Establish your metrics (average revenue per customer, close ratios, client loyalty, etc.).
- Forecast return on investment (ROI) for both individual sales efforts and your overall sales plan.
- Create real and meaningful new client generation goals.

Resource Checklist of Questions to Ask Yourself

This list is not meant to be all-inclusive, and not all questions will apply to you. However, we've found that these questions help people to think about important sales topics and succeed with goal planning.

How's My RASP?

- Am I ready to succeed with sales?
- Am I taking the right actions to succeed? (Get appropriate feedback.)
- What are the top-selling skills I need to improve to be more successful? Am I taking steps to get those skills?
- Am I following the right sales process to succeed?

Desire and Commitment

- Do I desperately want to achieve my stated outcomes?
- Am I willing to do what it takes to implement this plan and make it successful?
- What has held me back in the past regarding sales?
- Is there anything that I avoid or don't give my all to when it comes to sales that may hinder my success?
- How hard am I willing to work?

Sales Knowledge

- Do I have a firm grasp on everything I need to know to sell?
- Do I know my position in the market?
- Is my firm (or am I) well known, and can I leverage that?
- How can I capitalize on the firm's brand?
- What can I do to get known as a thought leader or credible expert?

Average Size of Sales

- Is my revenue per customer per year as high as it should be?
- Is the size of my initial engagement with clients too low? Too high?

Current Customers

- What are the untapped opportunities I have with current clients?
- What referrals can I get from current clients?
- Can I cross-sell to my current clients? Who else should be involved from the firm as I develop this client?
- Is my relationship with current clients as strong as it can be? How do I know?
- Can I replace my less-desirable clients (i.e., too low revenue or margin) with others?

Referral Sources

- Are there any partnerships I can establish to generate leads or clients?
- Do I have established partnerships? Am I getting the most I can from them?

Strategy for the First Sale

- Do I have a way for customers to experience my value without going full steam ahead right away? Do I need to do this, or should I get them to go full steam ahead right away?
- What is the best area for me to focus on to generate initial discussions?
- Do people know how to get started with me?

Lead Generation

- What's worked for me thus far?
- What tactics should I use to generate new discussions?
- Am I handling the first conversation the right way?
- How do my colleagues generate new opportunities?

Conversations and Closing

- Are my sales conversations as compelling as they should be?
- Do I propose at the right time?
- What can I do to improve my closing process?

Resources

- Are there any resources at my company that I can leverage (e.g., speaking opportunities, marketing staff, association memberships)?
- Do I have specific connections in my industry or my target's industry I can leverage?
- What special resources do I have that I can put to better use (e.g., mailing or e-mailing list)?
- Do I have a sales/entertainment budget? Do I need one?
- Do I know what it's going to take to get done what I need to get done?

Chapter 12 Tips for Leading Rainmaking Conversations

Discussion Letter Example

Dear Mary,

It was great speaking with you yesterday at our office about tackling some of the technology issues you're experiencing. In this letter, I'll outline my understanding of the issues at hand, and confirm our agreed-upon next steps.

As a law firm with 50 lawyers, your team spends the great majority of their day at their computers. With the recent turnover of your IT leader, you're exploring the possibility of outsourcing all of your IT to us, thus not going through the process of replacing your internal IT staff.

As you consider your options, key issues include:

- As you're currently without technology support (which you've historically paid approximately $120,000 per year in salary, benefits, and overhead), you have to make a decision quickly so your team will lose as little time as possible to technology frustrations and challenges.

- You expect to hire 5 to 10 new lawyers in the next 12 months, and will need to support them as you hire them.
- You have had catastrophic server failures in the past few years that have cost approximately $150,000 in lost billable time per instance.
- Average response time to technology support requests take too long.
- Past IT staff at your firm had strengths and weaknesses in various technologies that hindered your ability to operate efficiently and compete.

We are confident that we can help you solve these issues and, additionally, impact your firm positively in a few ways, including:

- Costs for working with us will be less than rehiring an IT leader.
- We'll be able to begin service for your whole firm within 24 hours.
- Average response time to issues will be immediate should you choose to work with us.
- We'll increase the protection and security of your servers significantly over your past efforts.
- We'll be able to support all of your new staff as you hire them without requiring you to hire additional IT staff to support them.
- As we have 40 people on our staff, we have experts in more than 20 different technologies that law firms use regularly. We'll be able to provide the broad base of expertise you've been missing.

As we work with more than a dozen law firms now, our experience in the area is quite deep. I've attached several pages from our web site, including a law firm case study (www.exampletech.com/lawcase), that you can read. Working with more than 100 businesses to support their technology allows us to stay on top of the world of technology and apply that knowledge and insight to help you.

It seems that there's a fairly compelling case to continue the discussion, and to get down to the specifics of how we might work with you. You said in our discussion that your COO, Montgomery

Scott, will need to be involved in the process from here forward, and that you'd check his schedule later today.

Once we schedule the meeting, I'll move forward with researching the three specific technologies you were interested in implementing. That will give you a sense of what it's like to work with us to make technology decisions as well as support your users.

I'll call you Wednesday to find a time that all of our schedules match up.

Best regards,
Katherine

Chapter 13 Prospecting by Phone: Creating Rainmaking Conversations

Visit www.rainsalestraining.com/booktools to download a Cold Calling Checklist that will help you plan and secure appointments with prospects by using the phone.

Checklist: Appointment Setting through Cold Calling

Use this checklist to make your calling process as smooth and effective as possible—from start to finish.

Plan Ahead

Know the value proposition for the prospect for attending a meeting with you. It isn't enough just to introduce them to your services. You need to have the WIIFM (What's In It For Me) for simply attending the meeting.

- ☐ Start with needs
- ☐ Talk to your current clients
- ☐ Don't use marketing-speak
- ☐ Test out a straw man
- ☐ Evaluate what resonates and what doesn't

Make sure your call list is prepared and ready to go. The right list is more important than the right style. Think carefully about who you are targeting for these conversations.

- ☐ What titles?
- ☐ What industries?
- ☐ What buying influence?
- ☐ What geography?
- ☐ What specific companies?
- ☐ What spending power?

Carve Out Your Selling Time and Make It Sacred

- ☐ Quantify the potential value to your firm.
- ☐ Commit yourself to follow through.
- ☐ Make the first call, and continue from there.

Assign a Goal for the Day or Calling Block, and Make Sure It's Achievable

When reaching C-level people, plan to call very early or after 6:00 PM. Know what you are going to say when:

- ☐ A real person picks up.
- ☐ The administrative assistant picks up.
- ☐ No one picks up and you get a voice-mail recording.

Practice Your Calls

- ☐ Select a cold or warm call you need to make soon.
- ☐ Script out the call using the appropriate call formula in the Cold Calling Worksheet. Listen to "What to Say During a Cold Call" for additional advice.
- ☐ Practice with a colleague, friend, or other trusted person.

Immediately before the Call

- ☐ Exercise your voice before the first call.
- ☐ Have calendar dates ready for the meeting.
- ☐ Call in blocks to get on a roll. Pick a number (i.e., make 10 calls in a row).

During the Call

- ☐ Take only 20 to 25 seconds (or less) to introduce yourself and state the reason for your call. Get to the point quickly.
- ☐ Don't try to give too much information on the first call.
- ☐ Project confidence. Remember, you're speaking colleague-to-colleague. Don't apologize for calling them.
- ☐ Give yourself energy. Stand up if you need it.
- ☐ Talk slowly in order to be understood.
- ☐ Don't read word for word from a script, and don't copy-speak. Be genuine!
- ☐ Ask for a meeting on specific dates, and don't just ask, "Would you like to meet with me?"
- ☐ Listen! It's easy to misinterpret what people say. Make sure you communicate well and listen to your prospect when he talks.

After the Call

- ☐ Record the date and time that you called the person, even when you don't reach them.
- ☐ Think about the call that just happened: Is there anything you'd do differently? How do you feel it went? Think about what's going on, and learn.
- ☐ If you have regrets about the call you just made, then shake it off. Learn from your mistakes, try to improve, and don't let it stop you from getting back on the horse and dialing your next prospect.
- ☐ If you're at the end of a calling block, take a break. Walk outside, grab a bite, rest, and get ready to come back refreshed.

General Guidelines for Success

☐ Make sacred selling time—and stick to it. You need consistency to improve and to measure your results.

☐ If you're procrastinating, STOP! And start making calls. Cold calling may or may not feel right for you, but to set appointments it works well.

☐ Don't stop until you've made all your calls. Keep dialing. Getting appointments is partly a numbers game.

☐ Be genuine when you speak with people.

☐ Keep in mind the more pleasant conversations you've had. You may get the occasional unpleasant person, but the majority of people in the world are respectful.

☐ Integrate cold calling with mail or other ways of contacting people and you will increase your response rate.

11 Places for List Building

There are a number of ways to build target lists. Here are 11 sources that can help you.[1]

NetProspex: Good for gathering individual contact information. Most of the content is user-generated, so it's less likely to have all of the companies and contacts you're looking for. Most contacts also have an e-mail address.

Zoominfo: Larger database than NetProspex. Also good for gathering individual contact information.

Hoovers: Good for presales call preparation. Rich information about company history, background, and senior contacts at a wide variety of companies.

InsideView: Good for targeting companies based on trigger events. Allows you to set watch lists, monitor editorial sources and social

---

[1] Thank you to Ruth P. Stevens for providing her thoughts on several of these list building sources. For more information, check out her annual review of the quantity and quality of B-to-B data sources at: www.ruthstevens.com/white_papers.html.

media activity, and to know what's going on in particular companies.

SalesGenie: Good for campaigns (list selection, for contact by mail or phone) to a broad array of companies in just about every industry. Likely to have every firm, but less likely to provide a large number of contacts at each company.

LinkedIn: Member names are not made available in bulk for marketing campaign purposes. For prospecting, or for other one-to-one outreach, LinkedIn is an unparalleled source of up-to-date information on individual contacts.

Industry Associations: Tend to offer a broad selection of members and subscribers in various specialties. Names are likely to be fresh and current, but there is no comprehensive coverage. Associations may rent lists and often restrict use (e.g., one-time marketing contact, no appendix of information to your database, limited selection criteria).

Demandbase: Good for building contact or marketing list. Contact info includes e-mail, phone, and business details.

Jigsaw: Good for gathering individual contacts at various firms, because the file is built by crowd-sourced sharing of business card data. Less likely to have every company you may want.

D&B: Excellent coverage of medium to large enterprise.

Harte-Hanks: Good for gathering contact information of IT decision makers, including telephone and e-mail. Provides specific information on installed technologies at target companies.

And Two Places to See How to Reach Them

Intromojo: Provides a mash of Linkedin, Google, and all the other information available about a prospect on the web. If you know the name of the person you are targeting, this will help you to find the right way to get connected.

PeopleMaps: Shows you the shortest distance from you to the person you want to meet. Takes the concept of six degrees of separation to the max.

Chapter 16 What You Need to Know to Sell

Although in the minority, some organizations systematically create sales organizations filled with fluent sales knowledge experts. If you would like to learn how the leadership at top companies accomplishes this, visit www .raingroup.com/booktools and download the white paper *How to Build the Expert Sales Force: The Missing Link in Across-the-Board Sales Performance Improvement.*

Chapter 17 Sales-Call Planning—What to Know before Every Sales Call

Business Development Call Planner – Example

Date: <u>August 27</u>   Prospect/Client Name: <u>ABC Technologies</u>

Current Situation Description:

- *Introducing new product area to a current client on Tuesday at 11 AM*
- *Client has another provider for this service area*
- *I do not know if the client is happy or unhappy with the current provider*

Business Development Goals for this Client/Prospect:

- *Sell $18,000 of products to this client per year of the new service line, on top of the $45,000 on average per year in revenue we already receive from this client*
- *Continue to network with this client to find new potential areas of business*

Desired Next Outcome:

- *Get meeting with management team to discuss how they can get more leverage and success out of this area at their company with our new product*

Strengths (what's working in my favor):

> - *I have a 7-year relationship with client and management team*
> - *Our new product has several performance advantages over the competitor*
> - *We just delivered a project to this client that saved them $2 million in costs*

Vulnerabilities (what's working against me):

> - *There is a competitor—I don't know the current level of client satisfaction*
> - *This product is new even though our relationship with the client is long-standing*
> - *A new person has taken over as CEO of the client company —I may need to do some reestablishing of the relationship*

Next Actions:

> - *Prepare my knowledge and my marketing materials in the new product area*
> - *Ask my assistant to confirm the meeting*
> - *Send an e-mail the day before the meeting outlining the new product advantages*
> - *At the Tuesday 11am call, find out situation regarding current provider*
> - *Ask questions based on areas where I know we have a strong advantage*
> - *Generate enough interest to get the management group to meet with me*
> - *Build rapport with the new CEO, and begin my relationship with her*

Business Development Call Planner – Blank

Date: _____   Prospect/Client Name: _____

Current Situation Description:

Business Development Goals for this Client/Prospect:

Desired Next Outcome:

Strengths (what's working in my favor):

Vulnerabilities (what's working against me):

Next Actions:

Appendix and Online Resources

Additional Resources to Enhance Your Sales Skills

There is a wealth of sales knowledge available through the many bloggers, thinkers, and writers who regularly can add to your always staying on top of your sales game. We have listed some of our favorites below.

Blog Name	Address	Blog Author
Understanding the Sales Force	www.omghub.com	Dave Kurlan
SellingPower	blog.sellingpower.com	Gerhard Gschwandtner
Steel on Sales	davidsteel.typepad.com	David Steel
Beating Feast or Famine	www.michaelwmclaughlin.com	Michael McLaughlin
B2B Lead Generation Blog	blog.startwithalead.com	Brian Carroll
International Business Blog	www.cindyking.biz/blog	Cindy King
Sales Machine	blogs.bnet.com/salesmachine	Geoffrey James
Sharon Drew Morgen	www.sharondrewmorgen.com	Sharon Drew Morgen
Closing Bigger	www.closingbigger.net	Shane Gibson
The Sales Blog	www.thesalesblog.com	S. Anthony Iannarino
Simplenomics	www.simplenomics.com	Mike Sigers
Sales and Sales Management Blog	www.salesandmanagementblog.com	Paul McCord
The Pipeline	www.sellbetter.ca/blog	Tibor Shanto
Modern B2B Sales	www.bmarketo.com/blog/category/b2bsales	Marketo
The Salesopedia Blog	www.salesopedia.com	Clayton Shold
Selling to Big Companies	sellingtobigcompanies.blogs.com	Jill Konrath
The JF Blogit	www.thejfblogit.co.uk	Jonathan Farrington
Ian Brodie	www.ianbrodie.com	Ian Brodie
The Science and Art of Selling	www.alenmajer.com	Alen Majer
Dave Stein's Blog	davesteinsblog.esresearch.com	Dave Stein
Cubicle Chronicles	www.tele-smart.com/blog	Josiane Feigon
Sales Lead Insights	www.sales-lead-insights.com	Mac McIntosh
Art Sobczak's Telesales Blog	www.telesalesblog.com	Art Sobczak
Gavin Ingham	www.gaviningham.com/blog	Gavin Ingham
Keith Rosen	blog.profitbuilders.com	Keith Rosen
Edge of Explosion!	www.danwaldschmidt.com/ideas	Dan Waldschmidt

Sales Marks	www.salesmarks.com	Jan Visser
Inside Sales Experts Blog	blog.bridgegroupinc.com	Trish Bertuzzi
Inside Sales Tips Blog	www.vorsight.com/blog	Steve Richard
The Sales Operations Blog	www.salesoperationsblog.com	Marci Reynolds
Hunting Big Sales	www.huntingbigsales.com	Tom Searcy
B2B Sales Lounge	www.b2bsaleslounge.com	Jeff Ogden
Fill the Funnel	www.fillthefunnel.com	Miles Austin
Kahle Way B2B Sales Blog	www.davekahle.com/salesblog	Dave Kahle
Partners in Excellence	www.partnersinexcellenceblog.com	Dave Brock
Harding & Co. Blog	www.hardingco.com/blog	Ford Harding
The Funnelholic	www.funnelholic.com	Craig Rosenberg
Sales Gravy—Jeb's Blog	www.salesgravy.com/jebsblog	Jeb Blount
Meeting to Win	blog.meetingtowin.com	Jill Myrick
Informed Innovation	blog.innovativeinfo.com	John Cousineau
Sales Playbook	www.yoursalesplaybook.com	Paul Castain
This Day in Sales	www.salesdujour.com/this-day-in-sales-blog	Gary Hart
The Accidental Negotiator	www.theaccidentalnegotiator.com	Jim Anderson
The Brooks Group Sales Blog	www.brooksgroup.com/blog	Jeb Brooks
Make What You Say . . . Pay	www.annemiller.com/blog	Anne Miller
Sell More & Work Less	www.engageselling.com/blog	Colleen Francis
New Sales Economy	www.newsaleseconomy.com	Chad Levitt
A Sales Guy	www.asalesguy.com	Jim Keenan
Fearless Selling	www.fearlesssellingblog.com	Kelley Robertson
Your Sales Management Guru	www.yoursalesmanagementguru.com	Ken Thoreson
Sales Training Advice	www.salestrainingadvice.com	Josh Hinds
Trust Matters	www.trustedadvisor.com/trustmatters	Charles Green
Keith Ferrazzi	www.keithferrazzi.com	Keith Ferrazzi
Eyes on Sales	www.eyesonsales.com	Various
SalesLeadership	blog.salesleadershipdevelopment.com	Colleen Stanley
Alan's Blog	www.contrarianconsulting.com	Alan Weiss
Building Enduring Client Relationships	www.andrewsobel.com/blog	Andrew Sobel
Hello My Name is Blog	www.hellomynameisblog.com	Scott Ginsberg

Mark Satterfield's Blog	gentlerainmarketing.typepad.com/blog	Mark Satterfield
Webinknow	www.webinknow.com	David Meerman Scott
Book Yourself Solid Blog	www.bookedsolidu.com/blog	Michael Port
The Sales Management Minute	www.salesarchitects.net/salesminute.php	Lee Salz
Jeffrey Gitomer's Sales Blog	www.salesblog.com	Jeffrey Gitomer
Wendy Weiss' Blog	www.wendyweiss.com/blog	Wendy Weiss
Selling to Consumers Blog	blog.sellingtoconsumers.com	Skip Anderson
Changing Minds	www.changingminds.org/blog/blog.html	David Straker
SalesBlogcast	www.salesblogcast.com	Doyle Slayton
CanDoGo	www.candogo.com	Various
SalesDog.com	www.salesdog.com	Various
Leadership & Learning	blog.kevineikenberry.com	Kevin Eikenberry
Buzz Marketing for Technology	www.pauldunay.com	Paul Dunay
Shift	www.shiftselling.com	Craig Elias

About RAIN Group

RAIN Group is a sales performance improvement company. Located in greater Boston, RAIN Group's focus is on sales training, assessment, and performance improvement to help leading organizations improve sales results.

RAIN Group has helped tens of thousands of salespeople in hundreds of organizations increase their sales significantly.

RAIN Group helps organizations:

- Enhance sales skills and improve sales results
- Increase cross- and up-selling success
- Recruit, hire, and retain the best sales reps
- Greatly reduce the learning curve for new hires
- Increase the success of new product and service launches

Since 2002, RAIN Group leaders and consultants have produced rigorous benchmark research resulting in publications such as *Fees and Pricing Benchmark Reports*, *What's Working in Lead Generation*, *How Clients Buy*, and *Professional Services Marketing*.

RainToday.com, the largest online magazine and membership site in the world focused on sales, marketing, and business growth for service businesses, the RainMaker Blog, and the RAIN Selling Blog are published by RAIN Group.

To learn more about RAIN Group, go to www.RainGroup.com

About
RainToday.com

Published by RAIN Group, RainToday.com is the largest online magazine in the world focused on sales, marketing, and growth for service businesses. RainToday.com's offerings include:

- Membership: RainToday.com Annual Membership brings you the freshest insights, tools, and advice to help you grow your service business.
- Free newsletter with articles by well-respected marketing, sales, and business experts such as John Doerr, Mike Schultz, Jill Konrath, Michael McLaughlin, Andrew Sobel, Bruce W. Marcus, and Charles Green on core topics in selling and marketing professional services.
- Best practice and benchmark research such as, *What's Working In Lead Generation, How Clients Buy*, and *Fees and Pricing Benchmark Report* by analysts and experts at RainToday.com.
- Case studies on what's working in marketing and selling services.
- Podcast interviews with world-renowned marketers, rainmakers, and business leaders.
- Premium content, templates, and tools designed specifically for helping service businesses to grow.
- Webinars, seminars, and events for rainmakers and marketers.

RainToday.com
Membership

Membership brings you insights, tools, and advice to help you grow your service business. With annual membership you have unlimited access to exclusive members-only premium content, how-to guides and tools, case studies, webinars, and more. Learn more: www.RainToday.com/StartYourMembership.cfm

Rainmaker Report—Free Weekly Newsletter

Rainmaker Report, RainToday.com's free weekly newsletter, provides proven tips and tactics to market and sell services from rainmakers, leaders, and marketers worldwide. Visit www.RainToday.com to subscribe.

RainToday.com Research

The RainToday.com research team produces best practices and benchmarking research to help sales professionals, marketers, and leaders to grow their businesses. The RainToday.com research team delivers custom market and client research studies for individual organizations.

For a complete list of available research titles visit: www.RainToday.com/Research.cfm

About the Authors

Mike Schultz, Co-President, RAIN Group

Co-president of RAIN Group Mike Schultz is world-renowned as a consultant and expert in sales training and performance improvement. Mike has worked with organizations such as John Hancock, Ryder, Quintiles, and dozens of others to improve sales performance and develop rainmakers. Along with his client work, Mike delivers dozens of keynotes and seminars per year for clients and leading industry conferences. Under Mike's leadership, RAIN Group was recently listed in *Inc.* magazine's list of the fastest growing companies in the country.

Mike is publisher of RAIN Group's RainToday.com, one of the world's largest online magazines (more than 100,000 subscribers) and membership sites for sales and marketing. He is also on the faculty in the marketing division of Babson College.

Along with the books *Professional Services Marketing* and *Rainmaking Conversations*, Mike has written hundreds of articles, case studies, research reports, and other publications in the areas of selling and marketing, writes for the RAIN Selling Blog, and produces RainToday's popular podcast series. Mike's thought leadership has been published, and he's been quoted as an expert, in magazines and news outlets around the globe, including *Business Week, Entrepreneur, Selling Power,* and *Sales and Marketing Management.*

Mike is an avid fly-fisherman and golfer, and actively studies and teaches the traditional martial arts of Seirenkai Karate and Jujitsu, holding the ranks of third-degree black belt and Sensei. He lives on a lake west of Boston.

John Doerr, Co-President, RAIN Group

As co-president of RAIN Group, John Doerr draws on an extensive career in business leadership, which has included senior executive management, sales and marketing, and product and service development.

John has taught and coached thousands of sales professionals, helping them become top-performing salespeople through in-house training and public presentations, both domestically and abroad. He has worked with organizations such as PRTM, London Business School, DHL, Informatica, and dozens of others to improve sales performance. Under John's leadership, RAIN Group was recently listed in *Inc.* magazine's list of the fastest-growing companies in the country.

John speaks on the subject of sales and marketing for clients and conferences throughout the world, and is a frequent guest lecturer at Bentley University and Babson College. As a leader and rainmaker, John has sold millions of dollars of products and services to some of the world's most prestigious organizations.

John's international experience includes four years in Brussels, Belgium, where he was managing director of Management Centre Europe, the largest pan-European management development and training services firm in Europe. In addition, he has consulted and spoken at numerous events in Europe, including a three-year run as chair of Management Center Turkiye's Human Resources Conferences in Istanbul.

John is an avid runner and two nights a week can be found skying for rebounds (well, reaching with great success and aplomb) on the basketball court with Over the Hill Basketball, Inc, an organization dedicated to men over forty living out their dreams of athletic achievement.

Index

Desire
  phase, 156
  principle of, 118
Disconnected buyers, 52
Domino strategy, 124

Effectiveness concept, 13
Effortful processing, 233
Eisenhower, Dwight, 146
Emotional impact
  clarification of, 76
  defined, 72
  ROI and, 121–122
Emotional journey, principle of,
    119–120
Engagement point, 143–144
Envy, principle of, 119
Espoused theory, 235
Expectations, knowledge of, 208
Experience, 171
Explicit needs, 157
Exploration, 104
Exploratory discussions, 215

FAINT
  closing and, 199
  components of, 162–163
  determination of, 147–150
  as objection response, 190
Financial capacity
  determination of, 149–150
  factors influencing, 75
  in FAINT, 162
  objections and, 184, 188–191
Financing, 191
Firms
  accounting, 60
  agendas, 100
  capabilities, 209–210
  capital-intense, 40
  growing, 13

relevance, demonstration of, 56
  value propositions of, 208–209
First step approach, 165
Five whys
  in action, 110–111
  analysis of, 112
  benefits of, 107
  example problem for, 108–110
  starter ideas for, 113
  use of, guidelines for,
      111–112
Follow-up
  lack of, 23, 223
  to meetings, 151–152
  multiple, 22
  questions, 104
  scheduling, 67
Future seeking mode, 60–61

Genuine rapport, 5
Gerstner, Lou, 29
Goals
  core selling, 67
  crafting, 32
  living by, 31–33
  prospecting, 156–157
  questions for, 33, 216–217
  reasons for, 29
  reviewing, 31–32
  setting of, 30–31
Good to Great (Collins), 24

How Clients Buy
  cold call acceptance research in,
      159–161
  personal chemistry research in,
      52
  purchasing decision research in,
      208–209
Hsieh, Tony, 55
Hunter, John, 30

Free RAIN Selling Book Tools and Online Training Lessons from RAIN Group

www.RainSalesTraining.com/BookTools

Above and beyond the content of this book, we've compiled a number of **resources**, **tools**, and **free online training** to help you more quickly and effectively apply RAIN Selling to your sales efforts and take your selling to the next level.

Sales Tools and Resources

Sales Goal Setting and Action Planning Tool: Here are 39 questions and tools to help you set your sales goals and develop an action plan to reach them.

Cold Calling Checklist: Use this guide to help successfully plan your cold calls and secure appointments with hard to reach buyers.

The 5 Hidden Weaknesses: Use this tool to help uncover any hidden weaknesses that might be holding you back from reaching top sales performance.

Rainmaking Conversation Planner: This tool, complete with a practical example, will help you plan each and every sales conversation, making your sales efforts more successful.

Free Online Sales Training Lessons

For those of you looking to learn more about the key RAIN Selling concepts covered in this book, we've made available content from our flagship RAIN Selling online training program. This content is yours absolutely free when you visit the web site below.

Download Your Free Tools and Training

To gain access to these valuable resources and more, visit: www .RainSalesTraining.com/BookTools.